HAUNTED MUSEUMS & GALLERIES *of* CANADA

HAUNTED MUSEUMS & GALLERIES *of* CANADA

Andrew Hind

QUAGMIRE PRESS

The Publisher: Quagmire Press Ltd.
Website: www.quagmirepress.com

Library and Archives Canada Cataloguing in Publication
Hind, Andrew, author
 Haunted museums & galleries of Canada / Andrew Hind.

Includes bibliographical references.
ISBN 978-1-926695-31-0 (softcover)
ISBN 978-1-926695-33-4 (epub)

 1. Museums—Canada—Anecdotes. 2. Haunted places—Canada—
Anecdotes. I. Title. II. Title: Haunted museums and galleries of Canada.

AM21.A1H56 2017   133.1'2971   C2017-902961-4
                                             C2017-904406-0

Project Director: Hank Boer
Project Editor: Sheila Cooke
Front Cover Images: littleny/Thinkstock; den-belitsky/Thinkstock;
jessicahyde/Thinkstock.
Back Cover Images: den-belitsky/Thinkstock
Photos: pp. 10, 12, 16 courtesy Whitchurch-Stouffville Museum; pp. 55, 61
courtesy Andrew Hind; p. 66 courtesy Muskoka Heritage Place; p. 88 courtesy Maria Da Silva and Andrew Hind; pp. 126, 130, 132 courtesy Haliburton Highlands Museum; and p. 141 courtesy Bunker Military Museum.

Produced with the assistance of the Government of
Alberta, Alberta Media Fund.

Alberta
Government

PC: 32

Dedication

This book is dedicated to the staff and board of directors at our nation's many fine museums, who work tirelessly and without fanfare to preserve and interpret our history.

On a more personal level, I'd like to dedicate this book to Dr. Claire Jones and the staff at Mt. Sinai Hospital. I cannot thank them enough for their warmth and understanding, for going above and beyond in their care, and for making the dreams of myself and my wife, Nicoletta, a reality. You are a part of the family we are creating.

Contents

Acknowledgements

There are many people who contributed personal stories to this collection, and for their generosity and time I am grateful. Some requested that I not mention their names, but I have little doubt that their experiences were very real. I hope I have brought the stories to life for the reader as vividly as they were for the eyewitness.

I am also in debt to the staff of the museums featured herein. Some in particular stand out, including Beth Sinyard of the Elman W. Campbell Museum; Kate Butler of the Haliburton Highlands Museum; Sara White of Muskoka Heritage Place; and Marg Harrison and Dan Larocque of the Bunker Military Museum. Others who deserve mention include Catherine Crow, who provided information regarding the ghosts at Roblin's Mill in Black Creek Pioneer Village, and Maria Da Silva, who assisted with research for Muskoka Heritage Place.

I want to thank Hank Boer of Quagmire for his endorsement of this project, and my editor, Sheila Cooke, for being a joy to work with.

Finally, I want to thank my wife, Nicoletta, for putting up with my absences and the long hours I spent locked in my office writing this book, and most especially for bringing joy to my life.

Introduction

~

I have a passion for history, so naturally, I love museums. I know that every artifact tells a story, and I love discovering these stories first hand. But not everyone is like me. Museums have a reputation for being stodgy and boring, so crypt-like in their dullness that they might as well be coated with the dust of the ages. Museums have been sadly maligned.

How many of the misguided people who yawn at the thought of visiting a museum might change their tune if they discovered that shadowy apparitions lurk in many museums, tied there through unnatural connections to specific artifacts or to the building that houses them? Would they still consider museums to be stodgy and boring? Not likely. They would thrill at the idea of encountering something spine-tingling. *Haunted Museums and Galleries of Canada* introduces readers to facilities across the country where cursed artifacts, spectral evidence of the afterlife, timeless mysteries and other unsettling matters are all on exhibit.

I remember the first time I had an eerie encounter at a museum. My parents took me and my siblings to Black Creek Pioneer Village in Ontario almost annually growing up. The Fall Harvest Festival was a highlight on our calendar. During one visit when I was about eight, I recall being excitedly drawn to the towering grist mill. At one point while I was exploring the ground floor, I thought I saw a shadow fall over me. I turned around but saw no one. At the time I was frightened. It bothered me for days afterward.

Thirty-odd years later, I'm certain the experience was born equally of a child's imagination run amok and, likely, someone passing by the mill's open door, temporarily blocking the sunlight and casting a long shadow within. But what if I'm wrong? What if it was indeed supernatural? I'll never know the truth. What matters, though, is that the experience helped make that trip to Black Creek Pioneer Village a truly memorable one, one that occupied my thoughts and dreams for days after and remains vivid as one of my fondest-remembered family daytrips. I remain drawn to the grist mill to this day.

That's the power of a ghost story, or even the suggestion of one. It can transform an experience, allowing you to feel that there may just be a way to connect with the past in a way no exhibit alone ever could. So you see, museums and ghosts are complementary.

All museums are a treasure, but I especially like smaller regional or community museums because of the personal stories they tell. I also like the way they deepen a connection to a place. My parents took us kids to Sainte-Marie among the Hurons a number of times. They were great times that left a lasting impression on my young mind. Even today, whenever I happen to visit Midland, Ontario, for any reason, I can't help but feel the courageous presence of the martyred Jesuit saints Lalemant and Brebeuf. I owe a debt of thanks to both my parents and this living history museum for the invaluable gift of truly feeling close to a piece of history.

Museums, as you will see within the pages of this book, may not simply preserve historical artifacts. They are also the curators of Canada's nightmares, the archivists of its fears and the trustees of all things that go bump in the night in the province. These paranormal tales are fascinating, and they also tell us much about Canada's rich, sometimes tragic and even bloody history—a history that sadly isn't as well known today as it likely should be. Whether one believes in the existence of ghosts or not, these stories are an important part of the fabric that comprises the culture of Canada and its many varied communities, and they deserve to be preserved as much as the physical artifacts.

At many of Canada's museums, not every artifact exists in the records and exhibits that have been arranged for public education. Sometimes it's a lost soul that defies cataloguing, a ghost that is part of the stories the museum relates. Join me as I crack open my crumbling vault of truc ghost stories to reveal some of the many restless spirits inhabiting museums and galleries across Canada.

And I encourage you: visit a museum and experience its collection—physical and ethereal alike.

Settlers' Spirits at the Whitchurch-Stouffville Museum

~

As with many historic structures, spectres of the past are said to cling to the walls of several of the Whitchurch-Stouffville Museum's half-dozen on-site heritage buildings like creeping vines to mortar. It seems each of the historic buildings, which together make up a small 19th-century village, has a spirit all its own, the product of the successes and failures, happiness and heartache of the men and women who lived and worked within it. These ghosts seem to recognize that without the buildings for support, their tenuous grip on life will come to an end; they would inevitably wither from existence and disappear forever. The history preserved at this museum is probably closer at hand than most visitors realize.

On occasion, the spectral energy lurking in the cracks between well-worn floorboards seeps out to startle staff and guests alike. Look no further than the circa-1850s log cabin, which represents a typical first home of a pioneer settler family. The legacy of those who lived in it can be seen in the architecture: the adze marks on the broad-beamed walls made by the calloused hands of an immigrant farmer; the light area on the wall where there were once stairs leading up to the loft bedroom of little ones; and black scorch marks that reveal a past fire, probably originating with a stray spark from the woodstove.

The former inhabitants left their mark in another way as well. Some say that their spiritual energy has become ingrained

The mournful sound of a woman sighing deeply has been heard on occasion at the 1850s log cabin.

in the cabin, becoming as much a part of the building as the thick log walls and sawmill-cut floorboards. The mournful sound of a woman sighing deeply has been heard on occasion, and paranormal investigators have recorded at least two women speaking back and forth, though their words were impossible to make out in the faint recording.

A woman named Vanessa visited the museum on a chilly, rain-soaked day in October 2015 as part of a Halloween ghost tour. The tour group trudged through the rain-soaked darkness, taking shelter in the cabin. Vanessa was at the rear of the crowd and heard from directly behind her a woman's rasping voice— distinct, but somehow far off and cloaked with the cobweb of ages. She spun around but found no one. Startled, she sucked in long, cold breaths. When at last her racing heart slowed, fear was replaced by curiosity.

"I asked in a whisper if I was alone. If a spirit lingered there, I asked that she let me know by sounds or some other way," Vanessa recalls.

Suddenly, the air grew even more frigid. Her breath began to hang like frosty clouds in front of her face, and her teeth chattered uncontrollably. Convinced she was being touched by a long-dead spirit, Vanessa took out her cell phone and began snapping photos. What she saw stunned her.

"Streaking white lines flashed across several of the images," she explains. "Was it due to the paranormal? Had I encountered the spirit of someone who had lived within the cabin? I believe so because I couldn't find an explanation for those lines or for the strange voice I'd heard or the sudden, intense cold I'd felt."

None of the other members of the tour seemed affected whatsoever. But for Vanessa, it was a profound experience.

Numerous families inhabited the cabin over the course of more than a century, so there's no way of knowing who this spectral woman might have been. But it seems she has an unusually strong attachment to the building that extends beyond the grave.

During two separate sessions in 2014 and 2015, the Wellington County Paranormal Investigators (WCPI) uncovered evidence suggesting that the barn and Bogarttown Schoolhouse are infused with spectral energy as well. In the barn, audio recorders captured what sounded like a conversation going back and forth. In a separate recording in the schoolhouse, you can clearly hear an adult male voice sternly reprimanding a student for some unseen childish hijinks. Moments later, a child's voice responds—perhaps pleading his innocence. Later, the sound of a young girl singing is heard as well.

Excited by their finds, the team set up a motion-sensitive infrared camera in the school. Hours later, the camera was suddenly activated—but by whom, or perhaps by what? When the team reviewed the footage, the camera showed nothing that could have triggered it to record. Bugs wouldn't trip it—they don't have enough mass—and because the field of view was several feet off the ground, it couldn't have been a rodent. It was puzzling, and with no rational explanation, the team concluded that maybe, just maybe, it was triggered by ghostly activity.

Then, upon completing a lengthy electronic voice phenomena (EVP) session and just prior to leaving the schoolhouse, WCPI set up an audio recorder on a desk. Before exiting, one of

One of the last remaining buildings from the vanished village of Bogarttown, the old schoolhouse is a reflection of an era long past.

the team members thanked the spirit children. On playing back the recorder at a later date, the team excitedly discovered they could hear a child's voice replying "thank you" in return.

Although the log cabin, schoolhouse and perhaps even the barn may be inhabited by unseen spectres, there is little doubt that the elegant Brown House is the most spiritually active building on site. The Brown House was the home of James Brown, a follower of William Lyon Mackenzie at the Battle of Montgomery's Tavern in 1837 and a prominent figure in early Stouffville. Not much has changed since the mid-1800s. The house retains its original trim and baseboards, painted a darker colour and treated with wood graining to make them appear like expensive mahogany, as well as its unique built-in closets in the upstairs bedrooms—almost unheard of in those days— which were designed to fit into the eaves of the home to give the upper rooms almost full walls without the usual sloping ceiling of a one-and-a-half storey home (important in an era when homes with a full second storey were taxed at a higher rate). The house is considered one of the finest examples of Victorian architecture in the township.

It's clear that the Brown family had means. In the dining room we find a pair of celery vases atop the table. While such vases appear mundane to us today, they are in fact indicative of wealth; during the 19th century, celery was a delicacy that would be served between courses, with the foliage sticking up for a pleasing presentation. Walls throughout the home are covered with busy bird- or flower-patterned wallpaper, carpeting runs throughout the house, and on the wall is an ornate clock dating back to the 1700s—all suggesting wealth. Finally, off the kitchen is a steep set of stairs that led to servant quarters on the second floor where a maid or two would huddle in the cold, the only heat coming up the stairs from the kitchen below. Only well-established and prominent families like the Browns could afford live-in domestic help.

The Brown family consisted of United Empire Loyalists who fled the United States after the American Revolution and resettled in Ontario. William Brown acquired land in Stouffville in 1819, which passed to his son James in 1852. In 1857 or 1858, James replaced the modest home that stood on the property with a larger, more ornate brick home that better reflected his status as a prosperous, upper middle-class farmer. While the home is fairly typical of a mid-19th–century farmhouse, it is special in light of the history it represents and the fascinating individuals who resided in it.

The Brown House played host to a number of important community functions. James remained active in politics even after the defeat of Mackenzie's ill-fated rebellion and became an ardent supporter of the Reform movement (now known as the Liberal Party of Canada). He and his wife, Barbara, hosted numerous political meetings in their home. The Browns also hosted women's institute meetings, gatherings of the Old Boys and Girls Club of York, and in June of 1868, the Grand Temperance Celebration was held on the property, which included a picnic, a concert by the Sharon Band and a parade that started and ended at the Brown farm.

The most notable event occurred in 1877. James' son John was a community leader like his father. Owing to his expert penmanship, John was often asked to write important documents, among them the incorporation papers for the Village of Stouffville. The document was actually signed right in the dining room of the Brown House, undoubtedly with a proud James Brown looking on.

James lived in the house until his death in 1882 at the age of 69. He willed the property to John on the condition that Barbara was well provided for. The will stipulated that Barbara be given living quarters within the house, so she remained in the home, sharing it with John and his wife Ann Eliza, and their four children—Morley (born 1886), Cora (born 1888), William Ross Edward (born 1889) and Mary (born 1898)—until her death in 1899 at the age of 74.

Continuing in the footsteps of his father, John was a pillar of Stouffville society, playing an important role in several community groups. He was a vocal advocate of temperance and even led prayers when a priest wasn't available. And, like his father, John was a skilled and hardworking farmer who provided handsomely for his family. Sadly, John and Ann Eliza endured personal tragedy when two of their children, Morley and Mary (who was noted as having been "in delicate health since infancy"), passed away at relatively young ages—Morley at 34 and Mary only months later at 23—casting a dark pall over their lives and their home.

When John died in 1926, the house and attached farm passed to Cora and her husband, Leland Johnston. Because he had suffered from polio, Leland could not climb stairs to the second-floor bedroom, so the couple used the scullery between the dining room and kitchen as their bedroom. Cora and Leland were so devoted to one another that when Cora died in 1952, the grief-stricken Leland couldn't bear to move on. He kept his beloved wife's clothes laid out on the bed, as if expecting her to return one day. A few years after Cora's passing, Leland sold the home and all its contents, but the kind-hearted new owners allowed him to remain in the house for many years in an apartment consisting of the parlour and slip room behind. In 1965, Leland left the home for an apartment in town, severing the last link between the home and the Brown family.

In the years following, the home went through several families before ultimately being abandoned and left vacant. Finally it was donated to the Whitchurch-Stouffville Museum in 1984, where it was painstakingly restored and returned to its mid-19th–century appearance for a 1991 reopening.

Perhaps because of the varied dramas that played out within its walls, spectral energy is unusually strong in the Brown House. It has been reported that objects will on occasion move on their own, as if propelled by unseen hands, and strange noises

The charming Brown House played a significant role in the history of Stouffville, so it's only appropriate that it is at the heart of haunted activity at the Whitchurch-Stouffville Museum.

have been heard. People complain of bad smells and cold drafts in the dining room, neither of which have an identifiable source, and the small adjacent bedroom has a heavy feeling of grief and mourning. In the basement, closed to the public and piled high with artifacts not currently on display, some staff members complain of being intently watched by some unseen figure.

In an effort to provide enriching Halloween programming for the public, in 2014 the Whitchurch-Stouffville Museum decided to call in experts on the subject. Enter WCPI, back for a second visit following their investigation of the museum the year before. That investigation had yielded some compelling data, and the members had experienced some of the spectral activity for themselves.

WCPI was founded in 2010 by three individuals with a combined 70 years of law enforcement experience: Joe Cairney, Bruce McClelland and Russ Teeple. "We began talking about unexplainable things we had seen in our line of work and hadn't put in official reports out of fear of being ridiculed, then decided to found our own group to bring our real-life investigative experience to the paranormal. We're open-minded because of what we've seen, but we look at evidence with a critical eye and thoroughly explore all possible explanations for a phenomenon before labelling it paranormal," Cairney says.

Since 2010, the group has grown manyfold and has investigated almost 20 sites, including the Elora Inn, Harrison Theatre and the warship HMCS *Haida*. With their analytical approach and extensive experience in real-world and paranormal investigation, WCPI was the ideal group for delving into the spiritual problems bedevilling the Whitchurch-Stouffville Museum and the Brown House in particular.

During the 2014 investigation, two team members who were sitting on the stairs leading down into the Brown House basement watched as a pram creaked, as if some weight had been placed on it. Then, to their astonishment, the pram rolled a few inches across the concrete floor. Not long after, Val Whiteside-Cairney, Joe's wife and a talented intuitive, ventured into the basement. There she sensed a male presence that lurked out of sight in the shadows. "The spirit is attached to the land, not to the Brown House in particular. He may have inhabited the land before the Browns came or been associated with the land in some other way—a hired hand, perhaps," Val explains.

Val also had strong impressions in the small main-floor bedroom adjoining the parlour. At one point she entered with Joe and felt the presence of a woman who was appalled by Joe's presence. Reared with strict Victorian values, the spirit felt it was improper for a man to enter her private bedroom. Later, when Val was alone, the lone female presence was replaced by a crowd of apprehensive, sad spirits who were hovering over the bed as if in vigil. She felt certain the spirits were those of close family and friends who were replaying the emotional final moments of Barbara Brown's life.

Then there was a cacophony of spectral activity in the parlour, where staff had laid out a wicker casket. The casket, which is usually kept in the basement, was causing unrest among a throng of spirits in the room. They thought it disrespectful for the casket to be there when—from their perspective—Mrs. Brown had not yet passed away. "I heard them saying over and over again, 'Why, why, why is it here?' They were very upset. The noise was overwhelming," Val recalls.

I had the opportunity to participate in an investigation of the Brown House alongside the WCPI in September 2015. During that drizzly evening, several strange and unexplained events occurred in the home, and though not conclusive evidence of the paranormal, they nonetheless left everyone excited.

The strangeness began well before the investigation, while the crew was still setting up infrared cameras in several rooms. John, a relatively recent addition to the team and an active police officer, is not easily rattled or given to flights of fancy. While walking up the well-worn stairs to the second floor, he heard the formal glassware that is set up on the dining room table—ready, it seems, to host guests for a sophisticated dinner party—begin clinking together. The noise was distinctive, unmistakable. John hastened back down the stairs and into the dining room. By the time he arrived, the clinking had stopped.

Before jumping to conclusions, John checked to ensure there was no rational explanation for the noise. There were no open windows or doors that could have let in a rattling wind. John then tried to replicate the noise by stomping on the floor and stairs to see if vibration might have been the cause but heard nothing beyond creaking wood. Eventually, he had to conclude that he couldn't find a rational explanation. Perhaps it was spirits of the past enjoying a meal…

Later in the evening, when the investigators ventured into the small bedroom behind the parlour, they noticed a dent in the blankets on the bed that neither investigator had noticed before. In fact, they were certain the bedding had been pulled taut during the earlier walk-throughs of the home. Strange.

Upstairs, a child's toy, the kind that lights up and plays a tune when handled or moved, was placed as a focus item in the children's room. At one point during the night, the investigators were startled to hear music filtering down from the second floor. It stopped just as suddenly as it began, but the toy had indeed played for a few exciting moments. Had a spirit moved the ball in an attempt to communicate and make investigators aware of its presence?

For a number of years, Mike Couling was WCPI's tech leader. He not only actively investigated cases but also was in charge of overseeing audio and video feeds. Knowing the interesting history and varied paranormal phenomena of the Brown House, Mike eagerly jumped at the opportunity to explore the building for himself during the team's 2015 investigation.

Joined by Joe Cairney and Deb James, Mike ventured through the building, scanning left and right with his infrared camera. At one point, he found himself standing at the foot of the bed in the master bedroom, panning across the room with his camera. All was silent and still—as one would expect, but not what Mike wanted. He was just looking toward the nursery at the back of the room when something flew out of the darkness, hitting him squarely in the chest.

"The only way I can describe it is that it looked like a ball of white hockey tape about the size of a jawbreaker. It hit me solidly, and I heard it drop to the floor," Mike recalls. "I swore and was stunned because there was no one in the room who could have thrown something at me, but what freaked me out was the fact that we looked everywhere and couldn't find anything that could have hit me. There was nothing on the floor of either the bedroom or the hall."

Despite not being able to find the offending object, both Joe and Deb had heard the sound of impact as something hit Mike. Was it somehow a figment of collective imagination? Did their eagerness to experience something paranormal cloud their judgment? You might be tempted to think so, but it seems unlikely. How would three individuals have experiences that correspond perfectly with one another's stories? Also, how would you explain the thudding sound caught on audio, right before Mike swears in surprise? Something hit him, but what? No one knows.

During their investigations, WCPI captured a couple of convincing EVPs in the Brown House, perhaps the most compelling of which took place in the basement. After a seemingly unsuccessful EVP session, Val and a couple of group members wandered off into the workshop at the basement's rear, leaving behind the still-active audio recorder. During their absence, the recorder captured a voice that seems to be saying, "They're hiding in the back room." Want to judge the EVP for yourself? You can hear it on WCPI's website.

Building upon the success of these investigations in the autumn of 2014 and again in 2015, the Whitchurch-Stouffville Museum decided to host events both years whereby the public could join the WCPI team as they delved further into the location's paranormal mysteries. It was a means of both entertaining the public and, more importantly to the museum's mandate, engaging the community and educating them about the history of the on-site buildings. During these events, some participants found the veil between living and dead to be too thin for comfort.

One gentleman who attended the event in 2014 seemed highly skeptical of the existence of ghosts and confident anything paranormal was all a figment of one's imagination. He had been dragged to the museum reluctantly by his wife.

"It was obvious he didn't want to be there. He was the kind of guy, with his arms crossed and a bored look on his face, who was very skeptical of the paranormal," remembers Joe Cairney.

The moon was high in the sky when the tour entered the Brown House parlour. Suddenly, the skeptic gasped in fear. Something had just whispered in his ear. His breath came in ragged gasps and his heart pounded in his chest. The man stood still, ears straining for the whispered voice to speak again. It never did, but he knew what he'd heard, and it left him shaking in terror.

Joe noticed a complete change in the man's demeanor. He looked solemn and ashen; skepticism for the event and certainty that ghosts were hogwash were replaced with uncertainty and fear. Joe approached the man and asked what had happened, at which time he shared his chilling experience. "This man went from skeptic to believer in 30 seconds," Joe recalls, a hint of amusement in his voice.

Treina Miller participated in the public ghost hunting event a year later, in 2015, and she also had an experience that left her questioning her views on death and the afterlife. After entering the Brown House and descending into its basement with other excited members of the public under the watchful eyes of WCPI team members, Treina separated herself from the group.

"I went into the back workshop [a small room off the main basement] and walked all the way to the back of the room alone. When I turned around to walk back out, I heard a loud swish of air in my left ear and then a sigh. The sigh sounded sad and male. Or at least the tone was low. It was drawn out, maybe lasting the count of three. I walked towards the door and noticed there were four or five chains hanging over a sheet that covered a piece of furniture (it might have been a sled). For no reason, one of the chains was swinging. None of the other chains moved, and the sheet never moved. I never felt a draft and couldn't explain it," she recalled later.

Treina walked out of the darkened back room and into the basement proper, where she found the rest of the group gathered. In hushed tones, she told her mother, Steina, and friend, Pat, what she had experienced. The three of them returned to the back room, audio recorders on and hoping to witness the chain mysteriously swinging once again.

"Pat noticed the chain beginning to swing again. My mom asked it to stop, and it did slow down," Treina continued. "Two other members of the group came in then. We watched as the chain sped up and slowed down. We asked it to stop as we left the room, but it sped up and then suddenly stopped. The other two members of the group looked around to see if anything could have caused the chain to move but found no explanation. It was weird because it sped up and slowed down for no reason and sometimes seemed to respond to requests to slow down."

Because it seemed to respond to commands, and because no one could find a reasonable cause, Treina believes the chain was moved by spectral hands trying to communicate with her. In light of the wide range of paranormal phenomena reported within the aged walls of this history home, Treina may well be right.

Vivid examples of paranormal activity such as that witnessed by Treina are the exception rather than the rule. Indeed, some long-serving staff at the Whitchurch-Stouffville Museum tell me that they've never experienced anything even remotely as dramatic, that most experiences are confined to that undefined feeling of being watched, and—most importantly—that they are confident that any spirits that may indeed linger in the on-site buildings are benevolent.

The Brown House, like all of the buildings at the Whitchurch-Stouffville Museum, is invested with a great deal of history, and the spirits that reside within are a part of that history. The dead, it seems, refuse to give up their residency. Perhaps they are simply reminding us that these buildings were once the physical representation of people's hopes and dreams for a better life. At the Whitchurch-Stouffville Museum, the past may well be closer than we think.

See For Yourself

The Whitchurch-Stouffville Museum is a unique blend of living history museum, with its carefully preserved 19th-century buildings, and traditional exhibit spaces for displaying artifacts and interpretive materials. One hall is devoted to rotating exhibits, while the historic Vandorf Schoolhouse (the only building original to the site) hosts a newly unveiled permanent exhibit that traces the rich history of the community. There's also an engaging Discovery Room for kids, which plays an important role in toddler programs and children's summer camps.

Over the course of the year a number of popular events are held at the museum, including an authentic Victorian Tea in November, where guests indulge in plum pudding, tea, finger sandwiches and desserts; an antique and classic car show in August, with hundreds of showcased vehicles; and a Candlelight Christmas in December, which sees the historic buildings lit with candles and lanterns while guests enjoy choirs, holiday baked goods, a reading of "'Twas the Night Before Christmas" and a visit with Father Christmas. This museum is well worth the visit at any time of year.

Ghost Ships Maraud Offshore at L'Anse aux Meadows

~

She was made of oak, with a carved dragon's head at the prow and painted shields lining the ship's sides. The ship was long, lean and knife-like, a predatory appearance for a predatory ship. Men with long, fair hair crewed her. They chanted as they rowed, pounding out tales of mythic deeds and past glories. They were fierce men accustomed to killing and taking what they wanted. They were Vikings, and they had come to Newfoundland's shores. For nearly 500 years, Vikings terrorized the seashores of the known world. A millennium later, perhaps they still do.

The year was 2005. Richard remembers the day he explored the shores around L'Anse aux Meadows well. The sun shone, the sea was low, seabirds wheeled placidly above and the world was happy. Then he saw the Viking ship sail into view and heard the chanting echo across the peaceful waters. He was stunned, and with good reason—the Viking raiders were a scourge from the pages of history books, a part of Europe's Dark Ages 1000 years prior. Although no student of history, Richard knew what he was seeing couldn't be real.

And yet there it was, sailing relentlessly toward shore and the former settlement that has been recreated as a tourist attraction. A chill tingled the back of Richard's neck. He turned and hurried back to the National Historic Site, hoping to reach the sod-and-turf buildings before the ghostly raiders did. Somewhere along the way he looked back out to sea, and the ship was gone—seemingly swallowed up by the kraken or one of the other fearsome beasts the Norse believed lurked beneath the ocean's waves. Richard slowed his pace to a brisk walk, and when at last he arrived at the park he related what he had witnessed to a female staffer.

With a wink and a smile, she explained that the Vikings had never truly abandoned their short-lived settlement in Newfoundland. Their spirits linger, both on land and more commonly on the water nearby. These spirits, tied to the former Viking settlement, are some of the most ancient on the continent.

Tucked in a bay on the tip of Newfoundland's Great Northern Peninsula, amid rolling green hills and rugged coastal rock and gazing out onto the harsh, chilly waters of the Atlantic Ocean, sits L'Anse aux Meadows. It was here, about 1000 years ago, that the first European settlement in North America was established—almost 500 years before Christopher Columbus first cast his gaze upon the Caribbean.

The Norse "discovered" Newfoundland in the year 986 CE when an expedition from Greenland reached its coast and put ashore on the island for re-provisioning. Compared to the near-Arctic land they had left behind, this landscape was lush and enticing. The green meadows, the sheltering forests that offered ample timber for construction and plenty of game for food and furs, the agreeable climate suitable for agriculture and the streams alive with spawning salmon all captivated the Norse. Expedition leader Leif Ericsson liked the location so much that he decided to spend winter there and ordered the construction of a sod-and-timber hall. In spring, the Norsemen returned to Greenland with their ship's hold full of wild berries, dried fish and, most valuable of all, wood, which was scarce in Greenland. Around hearth fires, these explorers spread tales of the bounty of the new land they called Vinland ("Wineland," after the berries they misidentified as grapes), which influenced more Norse to make the journey to explore the island and discover its riches.

In 1009, Thorfinn Karlsefni led an attempt to colonize Vinland. Some 250 men and women established a small community near what is now the Newfoundland hamlet of L'Anse aux Meadows. The settlement was short-lived; ongoing conflict with the native Beothuks made it untenable. In 1013, Karlsefni and the other colonists abandoned Vinland and sailed for home, taking with them Karlsefni's infant son Snorri, the first white child born in the Americas. When they departed, they left behind houses, workshops and a small blacksmith's forge. As centuries passed, the buildings were reclaimed by the land and forgotten.

It wasn't until the mid-20th century that these remains were discovered—a find as startling as the Vikings' discovery of Newfoundland nearly 1000 years earlier. In 1960, archeologists Anne Stine Ingstad and her husband Helge Ingstad discovered Norse landing places along the east coast of North America and were led to the site of L'Anse aux Meadows by a local who had long suspected that the ruins of an ancient community lay buried beneath the sod there. What followed was an eight-year excavation involving archeologists from Norway, Iceland, Sweden and the United States who, together, discovered the oldest European settlement in the New World. The site was inscribed on the UNESCO World Heritage List in 1978.

Over the centuries, many people have reported hearing chilling screams and the sounds of a desperate battle in the woods near the abandoned Viking village. Before archeologists discovered the site and pieced together its story, locals had no idea what those terrifying sounds meant. Now, most agree that they are the battle cries of spectral Vikings and Natives, a people the Norse called *skraelings*, reliving a life-and-death skirmish some 10 centuries after the participants were mouldering in their graves. According to the Norse sagas, the two sides had many bloody clashes before the outnumbered Norse were eventually driven back to their homeland, never to return to present-day Canada.

One such skirmish between the two sides claimed the life of Leif Ericsson's brother, Thorvald, and gave birth to the oldest recorded ghost story related to North America. In 987, Thorvald returned to Vinland. He and his companions happened upon nine Natives napping under a canoe. The Vikings quickly killed all but one. He escaped, and soon large numbers of Native warriors attacked in retaliation. Thorvald was shot by an arrow and buried nearby. When Leif's other brother, Thorstein, who had not been a part of this latest expedition to Vinland, heard of Thorvald's death, he was determined to bring the body back home. With a crew of 25 men and his wife, Gudrid, Thorstein set sail for Vinland. A fierce storm drove them back ashore, however, and then disease broke out among the crew. Thorstein took sick and died.

As his body was being prepared for burial, Thorstein sat bolt upright and his lifeless eyes flashed open. Those present screamed in horror. Some ran, some were paralyzed by fear and all muttered prayers to their gods. Thorstein's jaw made a cracking sound and dropped open. A cloud of sour air escaped from deep within his swollen body. "Where…is…my wife?" he moaned in a voice as dry as fall leaves. "Where…is…Gudrid? I must speak with her."

Gudrid was summoned to her husband's side. Holding his cold and rigid hand, she listened as Thorstein spoke in a hollow voice. He told her she would soon remarry and have children, that she would be widowed a second time and then would build a church in Iceland and live the remainder of her long life as a nun devoted to God. Having said his piece, a second gust of sour air escaped from his body and Thorstein collapsed, his lifeless eyes rolling back in his head. He neither stirred nor spoke again, but his prophecy was later borne out.

L'Anse aux Meadows has no dearth of its own ghostly tales. Viking long ships, their dragon's head bows as fearsome today as they were to coastal communities of northern Europe during the pillaging heyday of these fierce warriors, have been seen off the Newfoundland coast by startled witnesses since at least the early 20th century. Icelandic folklore says that spectral long ships depart from Iceland each summer and head west for North America, though no one can be sure it's these vessels that menacingly approach Newfoundland's shores.

One gripping story occurred late one evening. A fisherman was in his seaside hut preparing the day's catch for sale. Suddenly, something caught his attention. He stopped working and stood perfectly still, ears straining. There it was again, a distant sound coming in off the bay: multiple oars dipping into the water in unison. He went to a window, ran a hand across the glass to wipe away the grime and peered out into the gathering dusk. As the man had thought, there were no fishing boats out on the water. In fact, there was nothing at all to see, save for the seabirds wheeling and shrieking. The ocean was still, with a light fog forming on the calm water.

Thinking his ears were simply playing tricks on him, the fisherman returned to his work. Moments later, he froze yet again when he heard a sound that caused his heart to race: a battle horn trumpeted across the water, threatening violence and death. The fisherman dropped what he was doing and raced outside. The fog was now a wall of white over the water's surface. Three Viking long ships slid into view. The vessels appeared to rest weightless on the ocean, and when the oars rowed they dug only into air. Their bows and sterns curled high and were tipped with carved serpents. The fisherman's mouth dropped open. What he was seeing was impossible. The Vikings were part of the ancient past, their bloodthirsty pillaging having been extinguished hundreds of years prior. And yet there they were, surging across the ocean in front of him. He watched with a mixture of fear and awe as the vessels passed by and then, moments later, were swallowed up by the fog.

The Viking ghost ships returned to the shores of Newfoundland decades later, and once again a fisherman working late into the gathering dusk was startled by their sudden appearance. It had been an exceptionally good fishing day, so he decided to stay out on the water later than anyone else. He came to regret the decision when the wind suddenly picked up and dark, angry clouds began to roil above him. A storm was brewing.

The fisherman knew time was of the essence. He had to get back to shore before driving rain obscured his vision and the waves were churned into white-capped mountains. His heart skipped a beat when the boat's engine refused to start; it turned over and coughed but wouldn't spring to life. The fisherman felt panic begin to rise when he looked up and saw the bank of angry clouds drawing relentlessly close. The wind whipped his hair and his boat rocked on growing waves.

Then he heard oars on the water and stood up to wave, hoping for rescue. His eyes grew wide at the sight of the approaching ship: it was a Viking ship, with square sails and twin banks of 12 oars. It sailed straight for him as if it meant to ram his fishing boat, the eyes of the dragon on the bow glaring menacingly down on him as if ready to strike a killing blow. Just before the blade-like vessel would have sliced through the fisherman's boat, it simply vanished. Incredibly, at that same instant his boat's engine finally caught. Now shaking uncontrollably with terror, the man raced for shore as fast as possible.

Legends of ghost ships crewed by the damned are common across the world's seas. The driving force behind the crew of most spectral ships is a bottomless hatred for all things living. The restless dead prowling the rotting decks of these ships seek souls upon which they can vent their undying malice. The ghost vessels of L'Anse aux Meadows are somewhat different. Despite being crewed by fierce northern warriors who in life marauded the oceans, these Viking vessels seem harmless.

See For Yourself

When the Norse left Newfoundland 10 centuries ago, their sod-and-timber houses decayed, but the ruins of the original buildings are still clearly visible on the landscape. What you see at L'Anse aux Meadows today is a reconstruction based on extensive research done by archeologists in the 1960s. The reconstruction paints a clear picture of how the buildings would have looked and how the Vikings lived during their short period as North American colonizers. The site consists of three major complexes, each one of which had a residence and workshops for craftsmen such as boat-builders and blacksmiths. The buildings were made of sod walls and roofs over supporting timber frames. Each building was outfitted with a simple, round firepit used for heating, cooking and lighting the house.

Costumed interpreters wander through these buildings, bringing their original inhabitants to life and encouraging visitors to try their hand at spinning fleece into yarn, threading a bone needle or pumping the bellows in a working forge to assist the blacksmith in making nails. For greater insight, take a guided tour; or, better yet, join the popular evening Sagas and Shadows program, wherein visitors huddle together in the kitchen of a sod building to listen as staff relate Norse myths and true tales from the Viking sagas.

The visitors' centre provides context for the significance of this ancient site. Among its exhibits is a replica of a Norse *faering*, a rowboat used to transport goods and people from the larger *knar* (merchant ship) to the shore or to travel short distances along the coast. You'll also see artifacts found on-site that, while small and seemingly insignificant to the untrained eye, provided trained archeologists with a window into day-to-day life in the settlement.

Finally, take some time to explore the sprawling 80-square-kilometre park to discover for yourself the beauty and bounty that drew the Norse there in the first place. There's an incredibly diverse landscape to explore, including bogs, rug-ged coastline and wildflower meadows. Take the 2-kilometre Birchy Nuddick Trail, which leads inland to higher elevations and incredible vistas out over the Atlantic Ocean.

Piety Meets the Paranormal at the Sharon Temple

~

Piety meets the paranormal at the Sharon Temple in the village of Sharon, just east of Newmarket. Shrouded from the outside world by a protective ring of trees, the temple dates back to the 1800s when David Willson's Children of Peace worshipped there and lived by an idealistic belief system well ahead of its time. Today the temple is a museum, seemingly time-trapped. Some startled staff and guests over the years have cause to believe that spirits of the settlers who helped establish this community remain behind, working and praying, long dead but seemingly ill at rest.

To understand the Children of Peace and their temple, you first have to understand their founder, David Willson. A theologian, hymn writer and political reformer, Willson was born June 7, 1778, in Dutchess County, New York. There was nothing in his upbringing to suggest he would have any lasting impact on history. The son of John and Catherine Willson, pious Presbyterians, he was raised poor and apprenticed to a carpenter at age 14 upon the death of his father.

In search of new opportunities and perhaps driven by a vision, in 1801, he and his wife, Phoebe, and their two sons, John David and Israel, moved to Upper Canada (as Ontario was then known). Phoebe was a Quaker, so they trekked north along Yonge Street, at that time little more than a rough trail hacked through the woods, to join a small community of Quakers in what is now Newmarket. The Willsons settled along the second concession of East Gwillimbury and took to farming.

All was idyllic for a time, but Willson found himself banished from Quaker society and ostracized by many of its members for his radical preachings during the War of 1812 and for his belief that Christianity should return to its Judaic roots. Driven by the power of his convictions, Willson would not be silenced. Accompanied by a few Quakers who supported his views, he formed the Children of Peace, a sect he likened to the Old Testament Israelites, lost in the wilderness fleeing a cruel and uncaring English pharaoh. Together, these settlers founded a village sanctuary where they could worship as they chose, a "New Jerusalem" as prophesied in the Book of Revelation. This village, appropriately, was named Hope (later, the village was renamed Sharon).

The Children of Peace determined to build an elaborate and highly symbolic temple at the centre of their community, modelled loosely after the biblical Temple of Solomon. Willson himself was responsible for the design of the building, which he claimed came to him in inspirational visions, but he was neither an architect nor a master builder, so he hired the services of fellow Children of Peace member Ebenezer Doan. Willson also outlined a very specific timeline for the temple's construction: since Genesis stated that the world was built in six days with a seventh day for rest and observing the outcome, then this temple should take exactly six years to build and a seventh to rest upon completion. Construction began in 1825, and the temple finally opened in 1832.

Built on a floating platform with a foundation less than 45 centimetres deep—not even below the frost line and yet structurally sound to this day—and supported by pillars resting on stone, the temple expresses the unique religious vision of the Quaker migrants who settled in Sharon and takes its inspirations from the Bible. Its three tiers represent the Trinity. The four central pillars identify the four virtues: faith, hope, charity and love. The square design expresses the need to deal evenly and fairly with everyone. The 12 lanterns represent the 12 apostles who went out into the world to bring the illumination of salvation, and the equal number of doors on each side indicates that all may enter equally. The same is true of the similar number of windows so the light of God can shine equally. The golden ball at the top of the building represents the world and its people and reflects hope and peace. Jacob's Ladder, a gently curved staircase, leads to the musicians' gallery above. As Willson was attempting to recreate Solomon's Temple, the Sharon Temple even includes an ornate Ark of the Covenant, and in the centre of the temple, a bible sits open to the Ten Commandments. When finished, the 20-metre-tall building completely dominated the landscape of simple pioneer buildings. It became the centre of both worship and society for the Children of Peace.

The Children of Peace were an unusual group that embodied many contradictions, making it difficult to gain a true picture of who they were and what inspired them. They were a "plain folk," former Quakers with no musical tradition, yet they not only introduced both vocal and instrumental music into their services but also went on to create the first civilian band in Canada and build the first organ in Ontario. And as with all Quakers they were pacifists, yet they were at the heart of the Rebellion of 1837, providing not only then-revolutionary principles to guide the movement but also a significant number of men determined to fight for the cause and hundreds of weapons forged in local blacksmith shops.

By 1851, the Children of Peace were reputed to be the most prosperous farming community in Ontario. They were ahead of their time in many ways. They built Ontario's first shelter for the homeless, established a land sharing agreement so all members might have access to farmland, founded the province's first farmers' co-operative and believed in the equality of all people—especially as represented by the vote—regardless of social position, gender, religion and ethnic background.

David Willson was the spiritual heart of the Children of Peace, so it's unsurprising that his death in 1866 signalled the beginning of the end for the idealistic sect. His son John David assumed leadership of the group, but the Children of Peace increasingly turned their back on their religious roots and became instead a "charitable society." By 1890, shortly after John David's death, their order was extinct and their unusual tenets abandoned. The temple sat vacant and slowly began to deteriorate. The future of the prominent landmark in Hope that had stood sentinel over its faithful for nearly a century was at risk.

Thankfully, in what was one of the first acts of historic preservation in Canada, far-sighted members of the York Pioneer and Historical Society acquired the building and renovated it to ensure its future. Turned into a museum celebrating the Children of Peace, it reopened on September 7, 1918: the traditional fall feast day of Willson's followers. In 1990, it was designated a National Historic Site.

Today, the Sharon Temple museum inhabits a tranquil 4.5-acre, park-like setting it shares with a number of other historic buildings relocated from elsewhere in the community, including Ebenezer Doan's circa 1819 house, a small cookhouse, an 1853 log dwelling and Willson's 1829 study. Visitors immerse themselves in the legacy of the Children of Peace. For some, the immersion is deeper than they could have expected. These individuals are surprised to make a spiritual—maybe even paranormal—connection with the legacy of those idealistic 19th-century people.

Visitors often comment on the peace they feel at the museum, specifically within the temple: an all-encompassing sense of solace that drives away stresses and worries. There is no hum of electricity, no sound of vehicles passing by, no residential noises—absolutely nothing to intrude upon an inner peacefulness that's almost divine. It's as if the building itself is intentionally blocking out all outside noises to create an oasis of peace and tranquility. When you enter the temple, all your cares seem to dissipate, replaced by a sense of calm and contentment.

Many people claim to feel a presence in the warm, natural light of the building. To some, it's a divine presence. Others, however, are certain the presence they feel is that of spirits of the Children of Peace themselves who refuse to abandon the sanctity of the temple that defined their lives. Those visitors have the distinct impression that they are not alone as they marvel at the building's unique architecture, climb Jacob's Ladder to the second floor or simply stand silent and motionless, soaking in the sacred serenity. Far from being frightened, these people find themselves inspired by and perfectly at peace with the spirits they instinctively sense are pious and completely benign.

Only on rare occasions is the silence broken—in a beautifully haunted way. Several times per year, tourists will tell staff they heard music in the form of soaring hymns and solemn chants while touring the temple. There is never an earthly source for this music, and some of the claimants aren't even aware of the musical tradition of the Children of Peace.

It's not just within the temple that the line between past and present becomes blurred. Spirits are felt, heard and even seen in several of the other historic on-site buildings. In the cookhouse, for example, visitors report hearing unseen women talking and laughing, as well as the rattling of pots and pans as the spirits prepare a meal. Sometimes, there's even the scent of baking bread. Women also continue to labour in the afterlife within the log cabin that once belonged to Ebenezer Doan's son, Jesse. A female presence is sometimes sensed around the loom, and once a visitor entered the cabin and was startled to see the loom being worked by invisible hands. Perhaps the spirit was equally startled by the abrupt appearance of a guest because the loom stopped as soon as the visitor entered.

The most spiritually active building, however, is the Ebenezer Doan House, a comfortable two-storey frame home. While Doan was a prominent figure in the history of the Children of Peace, it is not his spirit that lingers within the home he built. Instead, it seems the occupying phantom is—once again—a woman. She's been seen on a few instances: a young, attractive woman wearing a dark, old-fashioned dress. Despite her beauty, she bears a grim countenance. Her somber appearance and the black dress lead one to wonder whether she is eternally mourning the death of a loved one. Most frequently, this female wraith is seen looking out onto an unfamiliar world from an upstairs window, a silent vigil of sadness and loss. Some people who enter the home are assailed by a heavy, almost dark atmosphere.

Megan Houston, program and site coordinator for the Sharon Temple, gave an interview to author Terry Boyle for his book, *Haunted Ontario 4*. In it, Houston admits to being uncomfortable in the Ebenezer Doan House. She also shares the experience of a co-worker. Late one day, this woman found herself alone in the home, tasked with cleaning it before leaving for the evening. While vacuuming, she was overtaken by the eerie feeling that somebody was staring at her. She cautiously looked around and found no one. Yet still the hair-raising sensation of being watched persisted. Finally overcome with fear, she fled the building for the safety of the office, leaving her chores unfinished and the vacuum in the middle of the room.

Some visitors to the home hear a mysterious voice when no one else is present. Footsteps follow guests and staff as they walk up the stairs. Doors open and shut on their own. In October 2010, a woman and her daughter participated in a tour of the temple and its adjacent heritage buildings. They had just finished viewing the second floor of the Ebenezer Doan House and were the last to descend to the ground floor. Upon entering the kitchen, they heard a thunderous bang from the bedroom above. There was no one up there, so who—or what—had made the noise?

Zoe had always been intrigued and inspired by the Sharon Temple and had long aspired to see it for herself. Finally, accompanied by her six-year-old daughter, she visited the museum in 1998. Zoe was thoroughly enjoying the experience and found herself inspired by both the beauty of the temple and the ideals of its builders. She recalls taking photos of the interior of the Ebenezer Doan House and being so distracted by her enjoyment that at first she didn't notice that her daughter had wandered a short distance away. Standing at the bottom of the stairs, the pony-tailed girl had her neck craned and was chatting happily with someone on the second floor.

Zoe knew that imaginary friends were common and initially thought little of it. In fact, she actually found it kind of sweet. Now ready to leave the historic home, Zoe called for her daughter to join her. At first, the young girl refused. She told her mother that she was talking with a friend. Zoe jokingly replied, "Well bring your friend with you."

The girl giggled. "She can't. She's a mommy like you and lives here."

Zoe got an eerie feeling. Suddenly, what she had initially thought was nothing more than a harmless imaginary friend had become something unnerving, even frightening. Zoe remembers her heart beating like a drum in her chest and that a chill ran down her spine as she raced over to grab her daughter's hand to pull her from the building. Braving a quick glance up the staircase, she swears she saw a dark shadow darting back into the bedroom.

A couple of years later, Zoe got up the nerve to ask her daughter about the experience. The girl innocently explained that the phantom woman she met in the Ebenezer Doan House was very nice and friendly, and that she wasn't frightened by her at all. What did this woman look like? Dark hair, dark clothes and very pretty—a description that meshes well with what others have reported over the years.

Who might the mysterious woman lurking in the shadows of the Ebenezer Doan House be? The most obvious explanation is Doan's wife, Elizabeth Paxson, whom he married in 1801 and who bore him seven children before dying in 1874 at the ripe age of 91. Perhaps in death she returns to her youth. Alternatively, the apparition may be that of Sabra Frey, a young woman whom Doan wed in Savannah, Georgia, in 1795. Tragically, she died a mere year later. Perhaps she followed Ebenezer to Canada. Any theory is mere speculation. Regardless who she was in life, this ghostly woman bears such a strong connection to the home that she clings to it tenaciously in death.

John McIntyre, a former director of the Sharon Temple, heard many stories of people being on the historic site after hours and having paranormal experiences. In an article appearing in the Newmarket *Era-Banner* in October 2010, McIntyre explains he didn't always know what to make of those stories. The ghostly footsteps people spoke of might have a rational explanation, he reasoned. The building, after all, has stood for nearly 200 years, and there was always the chance the sounds heard were just those of an ageing building settling. Nonetheless, even though he's a scholarly man, he readily admits to being open to the possibility of ghosts. He reasons that too many people—young and old alike—were having experiences to be able to dismiss all of them and notes that many of the ghost stories he heard over the years made sense from a historian's perspective. "I'm actually a little jealous and wish I had one of those experiences myself," he said candidly.

More than merely a stunningly beautiful structure, the Sharon Temple relates a significant chapter of our pioneer past. It feels as if time has stood still there, remaining forever in the first half of the 1800s, when the Children of Peace were at their peak and the strength of their spiritualism was strongest. Does the strength of their convictions tie some of the Children to the temple and its related historic buildings even two centuries later? Visit the museum for yourself and see what you feel.

See For Yourself

The majestic Sharon Temple, nestled in its tranquil park-like setting with other mid-19th century buildings, is as close to time travel as one can experience. It's not hard to imagine your-self back in the 1830s, when the temple was a monument to the principles of the unique Children of Peace religious group.

On the grounds, you can tour eight distinctive heritage buildings. Begin with David Willson's study, a beautiful build-ing completed in 1829, where he wrote his hymns, sermons, books and pamphlets. Not far away is a frame cookhouse, where the congregation prepared their feasts. Next is the exhibit build-ing, where many of the museum's 6000 artifacts are on display, outlining the history of Sharon and the Children of Peace, as well the significant role the group played in the struggle for democracy, social justice and women's rights in early Canada. Beyond this building is a log house once owned by Jesse Doan, Ebenezer's son and bandmaster for the Children. Across the lawn is the Ebenezer Doan frame home, furnished as it might have been in the 1850s. Finally, behind the house is a cylindrical outhouse designed by Willson.

Guided tours detail the background of the Children of Peace, their activities in and influence on Ontario. There are many special events throughout the year. Perhaps foremost among them is the Illumination, inspired by the settlers' fall Feast of Illumination, when the Children placed 116 candles in their temple's windows to represent the light of the Gospel. Held the first Friday evening in September, the modern-day Illumination continues this tradition in what is a spiritually and aesthetically beautiful display.

Painting a Paranormal Picture: The Emily Carr House

~

E veryone has a mental image, born of Hollywood films and gothic fiction, of what a ghostly encounter is like. Pale fog clings to the land. A hollow wind shrieks through barren trees while somewhere in the distance an unidentified bird croaks tunelessly. Terror enshrouds your every step as you approach a derelict home with broken shingles on the roof and shutters tilted at all angles over cracked windows. The weathered house promises hideous torments and dread afflictions within. Climbing the creaking front steps, your limbs go numb and you tremble in fear as you reach for the grimy door handle.

But not every haunted house is home to a spirit radiating hatred and fury, and not every ghostly experience leads to nightmares. The Emily Carr House in Victoria, BC, is a museum dedicated to the life and work of that iconic Canadian artist, and it is a perfect example of how reality rarely meshes with fiction. A charming historic house surrounded by well-kept gardens bursting with lively colours, it is nonetheless thoroughly haunted.

Emily's father, English-born merchant Richard Carr, had the home built in 1863 on a large farm-like estate in what was then the heart of Victoria. Neighbours included merchants, businessmen and politicians—evidence of the relative wealth and comfort the Carr family enjoyed.

Emily was born in the home in 1871, the second youngest of nine children, and she spent much of her life there or within walking distance. It was a joyful upbringing that left a lasting impression on her, resulting in vivid memories she fondly recalled later in life. In her book *The Book of Small*, Emily offers a description of her childhood home and environs as they were around 1880: "Our street was called Carr Street after my Father. We had a very nice house and a lovely garden. As far back as I can remember Father's place was all made and in order. The house was large and well-built, of Californian redwood, the garden prim and carefully tended. Everything about it was extremely English. It was as though Father had buried a tremendous homesickness in this new soil and it had rooted and sprung up English. There were hawthorn hedges, primrose banks, and cow pastures with shrubberies."

Emily and her siblings were raised in a disciplined and orderly household with English Presbyterian values, including Sunday morning prayers and evening Bible readings. Despite being a staunch traditionalist, Richard Carr encouraged Emily's burgeoning artistic inclinations. Nevertheless, it was only in 1890, after both parents had passed away, that Carr pursued her art seriously. She attended the San Francisco Art Institute from 1890 to 1892, and then in 1899 she studied at the Westminster School of Art in London, England. Although she had undeniable talent, Carr spent most of the next 15 years running a boarding house known as the House of All Sorts adjacent to her childhood home. Her one real foray into art, teaching in Vancouver at the Ladies Art Club, ended in less than a month because of her habit of smoking in class and cursing at her students.

Emily's fortunes changed for the better during the 1920s when people began to take note of her work. Her paintings were exhibited throughout Canada, as well as in London, Paris and New York. Much of this sudden recognition can be attributed to the endorsement of the Group of Seven; Lawren Harris, one of the members of this loosely affiliated brotherhood of artists, told Carr, "You are one of us," cementing her position as one of Canada's most influential painters.

Emily became renowned for her painted interpretations of the Aboriginal culture, forested landscapes and rugged seashores of the Pacific Northwest Coast. Her paintings are so immersive that people who had never even visited British Columbia came to feel that they knew it. Emily Carr was also a favourite of the women's movement of the day because she had become successful and respected in an artistic world that was, at that time, largely dominated by men.

Sadly, Emily's health began to decline even as her fame was rising. She suffered a heart attack in 1937 and another one two years later. In 1940 she suffered a serious stroke, and in 1942 she had another heart attack. In these latter years, Emily's focus shifted from painting to writing. Her first book, *Klee Wyck*, a collection of short stories based on her experiences with Aboriginal people published in 1941, earned her the Governor General's Award for non-fiction.

Emily Carr spent the last few years of her life residing in Victoria's James Bay Inn, which at that time was a hospital and priory operated by nuns. She died there on March 2, 1945, after yet another heart attack. While she may have spent her last years in hospital, her heart never really left the beloved childhood home where she made so many fond memories.

But at the time of her death, this home would have been almost unrecognizable to Emily. It had changed dramatically. The expansive estate had long since been subdivided into building lots, while the house itself had been extensively altered by a number of expansions over the years and reconstruction after a devastating 1938 fire. The house passed from one member of the Carr family to the next for several years, never truly being well cared for, before being sold to a private owner for use as a rental property. By 1964, the historic home was in poor repair and in danger of demolition.

Thankfully, David Groos, Member of Parliament for Victoria, stepped forward to save the building; he bought it and turned it over to the Emily Carr Foundation for use as an art gallery and a school known as the Emily Carr Arts Centre. In 1976, the provincial government purchased the property and began a lengthy restoration to undo the many alterations that had been made to the house over the years. Using photos from Emily Carr's lifetime, the interior of the home was returned to its late 19th-century appearance, including wood finishes, wallpaper and perfectly matched paint schemes. While most of the original furnishings and artifacts had long since moved on, a handful of items have been recovered and restored, including the Carr family Bible, some of the original pieces of hardware for the doors and windows and the piano in the parlour, which was originally owned by a neighbour. Now a National Historic Site, the Emily Carr House is also a museum and interpretive centre for Carr's art, writings and life.

The home's restoration is so authentic, and the building so infused with fond memories of her childhood, that it's perhaps only natural that Emily's restless spirit would be drawn back there. Considered eccentric and enigmatic in life, she and her home remain so after her death.

Emily herself seemed open to spirituality and the possibility that there is an existence beyond our mortal form. As a child, she was something of a loner who seemed to prefer her own company or that of the farm animals on the property to other people. Her most faithful companion for a number of years was an invisible friend who accompanied her on her adventures, with whom she never fought and who had a personality that meshed with her own. This isn't particularly extraordinary as many children adopt imaginary friends, except for one detail: as an adult, Emily herself wondered whether her childhood friend was actually a ghost rather than a figment of her notably vivid imagination. "I always wondered," she wrote, "if it was the spirit of a young boy who joined me."

Many people believe it was this openness to spirituality and the unconventional manner in which she lived her life that have fuelled Emily's spirit to return from beyond the grave to haunt her childhood home. Strong-willed and unbound by convention, she'll pass over to the other side when she's ready to do so and not a moment before.

Artwork from local artists is frequently displayed in the museum's exhibit room. Surely Emily Carr would agree with the decision to offer exposure to aspiring artists; after all, it took decades for her work to gain any recognition. But Emily was said to have been a harsh critic in life, and perhaps she remains so in death. Sometimes volunteers would try to hang a new show only to be frustrated and startled as paintings flew off the walls and objects were moved around by unseen hands. Volunteers routinely blame Emily. Is she showing disapproval of the artwork in question? Maybe so.

Emily rarely allows herself to be seen. The closest she came in recent years was in 2015 when a couple from mainland British Columbia visited the museum. While in the building, the man, "Tyler," looked down to read an incoming text on his phone. His wife, "Sara," asked about the message, and when Tyler looked up from the phone to respond, he saw a dark shadow glide across the wall in front of him. The shadow was very pronounced and was distinctly that of a woman. Tyler spun around quickly to see who had walked behind them to cast the shadow, but no one was there. He became unnerved as the implication of what he had seen began to sink in: if no living person was there to cast the shadow, then it could only have been the shade of someone long dead.

Sara saw the colour drain from his face and was startled by his unusual behaviour. She hadn't seen the shadow slide along the wall and therefore had no idea why he had spun around so abruptly or why his face was ashen. What's more, she confirmed that no one living had passed through the room. Tyler is convinced he caught a momentary glimpse of Emily Carr's apparition.

On another occasion, a visitor captured on camera an orb hovering in front of the headboard of a bed in one of the bedrooms. Most reputable and serious paranormal investigators will tell you that the majority of orbs are airborne particulates, moisture or tricks of light. But this one, the photographer insists, was different than any she had captured before. First, it seemed to emit its own light while still maintaining a transparent quality that allowed the pattern of the headboard to be visible through it. Second, it seemed to give off a static energy—the woman remembers that as she approached the bed, the hair on her arms and head began to stand on end, and she felt warmth on her skin. When she stepped back, the energy diminished. She was excited and a bit unnerved. Never before had she taken a picture of an orb that had any impact on the material world.

Psychics have sensed Emily's presence in the home, particularly on the staircase; there the spirit demonstrates a strong emotional response. Psychics also claim Emily isn't alone in the house, but rather has been joined in the afterlife by her mother, who died in 1886.

Barbara Smith, the author of a number of books on ghosts and the paranormal, is one of many people who believe that the Emily Carr House is haunted, and not only by the famed artist. Her conviction isn't merely the result of the weight of evidence and the mass of testimony but also born of personal experience.

Smith visited the museum while researching *Ghost Stories and Mysterious Creatures of British Columbia*. Upon entering the historic home, she was greeted by a staff member. Smith immediately asked whether the building was haunted. In reply, she received an enigmatic smile loaded with unspoken meaning and was told to tour the home and return with her own impression. It was a reasonable enough request, so off Smith went.

"I thoroughly enjoyed poking about the main floor but sensed nothing out of the ordinary," she writes. "As soon as I climbed the stairs, however, I felt uncomfortable, as though I was intruding into someone else's space. Although my urge was to escape the sensation by retreating to the main floor, I'd waited a long time to visit Emily's birthplace and was determined to at least complete my tour."

Smith admits she is far from psychically sensitive, yet the weight of emotion threatened to overwhelm her. She was terrified and felt unwelcome, and only through strength of will was she able to continue exploring the building. She pushed on, coming next to the bedroom belonging to Emily's mother. Although the public is invited to step right into the faithfully restored bedroom, Smith found that she could not. Some invisible force held her back, preventing her from crossing the threshold.

"A sense that it was someone else's personal space was just too strong, and I went back downstairs immediately," Smith writes. "After waiting a moment to compose myself, I approached the woman I'd spoken to earlier. She smiled and acknowledged that Emily Carr House is indeed haunted. Apparently, as a youngster, Emily was afraid to climb the staircase at night. To ease the child's fears, her mother used to stand at the top of the stairs while the child made her way up. That anecdote certainly explained the protective presence that I detected as I climbed the stairs."

A wandering soul through much of her life, it seems Emily remains so in the afterlife. Her apparition has been seen in a number of other locations around British Columbia; her ghost refuses to be limited to a single locale. Most famously, she has made her presence known in the historic James Bay Inn, where she spent the last few years of her life and where she died in 1945.

The hotel opened to much fanfare in 1911. It was considered one of the most majestic hotels anywhere in British Columbia and a symbol that Victoria was outgrowing its reputation as a small provincial town. After decades of hosting wealthy guests in comfortable style, the building had a brief interlude as a hospital from 1942 to 1945. It was during this time that Emily

Carr, her health undermined by several heart attacks and a serious stroke, was admitted for long-term care. Emily passed her time writing and painting in the upstairs lobby, and she would occasionally take her art outside to sell on the street corner. She died in her room, the victim of one final, fatal heart attack.

Shortly after the building reverted back to a hotel, guests began complaining that they were roused from their sleep late at night by an ethereal manifestation of the deceased artist. A Canadian icon and a local celebrity, there was no mistaking the identity of the shimmering spirit standing over their beds, staring down on guests as they tried fitfully to return to sleep.

Other paranormal phenomena have been credited to Emily Carr's continued presence. Startled guests have received phone calls without anyone on the other end—literally dead silence—and when they inquire about it at the front desk, there is no record of incoming calls. Other guests have been awoken in the middle of the night by televisions that have turned themselves on with the volume raised to ear-splitting levels. No explanation can ever be found to satisfy the guests whose hearts are pounding with fear.

Staff members at the James Bay Inn have had their fair share of experiences with the next world intruding into our own. Sometimes beds freshly made will be rumpled or even unmade with blankets askew as soon as the cleaning staff turns their back for a few moments. Vacuums mysteriously stop working only to start working again just as suddenly. And then there was the time a cleaning woman watched as curtains fluttered even though there was absolutely no air flow, either from an open window or from an air conditioning/heating system. With hair rising on her arms, the woman raced from the room. As a result of these startling experiences and others like them, staff members keep one eye on their task and one eye on the dark corners.

Emily's ghost is not confined to the guestrooms. Her ethereal form is also occasionally seen in the hotel's pub and restaurant, where she has been witnessed passing through walls and once reached out to grab a bartender's leg from behind, causing him to literally jump in fright. Diners headed towards the men's washroom often shiver as they pass through an intense cold spot described as being like stepping into a walk-in freezer. Then, once in the washroom, they find themselves looking about uncomfortably, even glancing into stalls, unable to shake the feeling they are being intently watched by disapproving eyes. If pressed, staff will whisper that they know why: it seems that when the hotel was renovated, Emily's bedroom was converted into the men's bathroom. Perhaps understandably, Emily's spirit is aghast that men are relieving themselves in what she considers her living quarters.

But it's her childhood home where Emily's heart was, and perhaps remains, so if you want to feel a connection with one of Canada's iconic artists, that's where you should go. Immerse yourself in Emily Carr's life and work, but don't expect her to make an appearance. As she always has, Emily defies convention—she'll make her presence known when and if she wants, and in whatever manner she chooses. In life she wanted to be known for her artwork. Her spirit surely feels the same way, undoubtedly preferring to be spoken of for her artistic ability rather than the nature of her haunting.

See For Yourself

Located in a beautiful and historic oceanside Victoria neighbourhood near Beacon Hill Park, the Emily Carr House is an artifact in its own right and was designated a National Historic Site in 1964. The two-storey home is an excellent and well-preserved example of the picturesque Italianate villa-style homes popular among the wealthy classes in the 1870s. Architecturally distinctive features include a ground-floor veranda, high ceilings, round-headed paired windows on the second floor and paired brick chimney. The family home has been made up in lavish English fashion, with ornate mouldings, flowery wallpaper and other details that marked the home as that of a well-to-do family. In addition to the artifacts on exhibit and the heritage appeal of the Emily Carr House itself, the museum is surrounded by a charming Victorian-style garden that visitors love to explore.

In an effort to foster local arts, the museum also features a People's Gallery, where local artists inspired by Emily Carr and her work can showcase their own artistic endeavours.

No Cure for What Ails the Niagara Apothecary

~

No region in Canada has been as touched by the ravages of war as Niagara. During the War of 1812 it was contested ground, with the British and Americans fighting desperately for control of this strategic region in battles at Lundy's Lane, Queenston Heights, Fort Erie and Chippewa, as well as numerous minor skirmishes. Homes, farms and entire communities were razed to the ground. Thousands of people became refugees.

As a consequence of this bloody history, the Niagara peninsula is home to more than its fair share of museums haunted by the region's troubled past: McFarland House, the Laura Secord Homestead, Butler's Barracks, Fort Erie, Fort George, the Niagara Historical Museum and more. Within the halls of these museums, historic homes and battle-scarred forts, old animosities are renewed and the suffering of war endures. For good reason, Niagara is labelled the most haunted region in Canada.

Ironically, one of the buildings in Niagara with the most active spectral activity has absolutely no connection to conflict. The Niagara Apothecary, located in the heart of Niagara-on-the-Lake, was one of Canada's longest continuously serving drug stores—certainly it was the oldest in Ontario. Today it is a museum depicting the history of pharmacies in early Canada.

The building housing the apothecary began its existence as a customs building. Later, a promising young lawyer, Edward

Clarke Campbell, who would go on to prominence as a judge, hung his shingle from its storefront. In 1869, the building was purchased by Henry Paffard and remodelled to serve as a new home for his thriving drug store. Paffard, and the five pharmacists who followed in his footsteps, served Niagara-on-the-Lake by dispensing pills and providing medicines to the ill. It was a profitable trade, and an important one for the health and well-being of the community.

After nearly 100 years in operation, the pharmacy finally closed in 1964. Recognizing its historic value, the Ontario Heritage Foundation acquired the pharmacy, restored the building to its 19th-century condition and reopened it as a museum in 1971. The Ontario College of Pharmacists was brought in to ensure the museum accurately depicted an operating drug store in the 1860s. The College also agreed to oversee the operation of the museum. With their professional knowledge, they were a logical choice.

The result is impressive; the museum is a near-perfect recreation. Almost all of the fixtures, the black walnut countertop and even the store clock are original and date back to 1865. In addition, many early account ledgers and prescription books, as well as an impressive collection of jars and bottles from the old business, have been recovered and are now on display. The museum transports visitors back in time.

Although the Niagara Apothecary may not be one of the area's largest or best-known museums, it certainly ranks among its most haunted. One if its exhibits is a spectral pharmacist— a long-dead proprietor whose presence adds authenticity to the 19th-century pharmacy.

Since the day of its 1971 opening as a museum, staff members and visitors alike have noted strange events within the building. Oftentimes, early in the morning or after closing in the evening, creaking floorboards are heard overhead. The staff member pauses in his activity to listen to the distinct sound of footsteps treading across the second floor. Because he should be alone in the building at this hour, the sound alarms him. Has someone broken in? Is there a trespasser or thief upstairs? Cautiously, unsure of what he will find, the employee climbs the stairs, heart pounding. To his relief, upon investigation he finds his fear is unfounded. There is never anyone on the second floor.

Footsteps are also frequently heard on the very staircase the employees climb on shaking legs while investigating these mysterious noises. Generally it is just the measured pace of someone casually walking, but sometimes the noise is the heavy and hasty tread of someone running. Who, or what, are they running from? It causes one to pause and wonder.

The museum employees are mostly pharmacy students and historians—rational-minded individuals—so accepting the presence of ghosts can be slow in coming. Sometimes, it takes evidence. Once, several staff members decided to test for the presence of ghosts in what they considered an empirical way. Just before closing that night, they carefully placed newspapers over the steps. When they returned in the morning, the pages had been disturbed. With no breeze from an open window, no movement of air from an air-conditioning unit or fireplace, there seemed to be no logical explanation. The disturbed newspapers were proof, at least in their minds, that an apparition did indeed tread through the building after dark.

But footsteps aren't the only unusual phenomenon to unsettle staff members and visitors. Icy-cold spots in an otherwise warm building are a common complaint, and there have been reports of unusual flashes of light near the back of the building. And then there is the smell of belladonna that many people notice. Also known as deadly nightshade, this herb is no longer kept on the premises—despite being an authentic 19th-century curative—because of the danger it poses if ingested. So, if there is no belladonna on site, what is the source of this distinctive smell? Is it an olfactory echo of the past?

A rare few individuals have seen the apparition. He is described as a distinguished-looking older man, tall and straight-backed despite his age and dressed in a black suit and hat. He tends to appear only momentarily and typically looks like a flesh-and-blood person—until he fades from view or disappears through a wall.

A family visiting Niagara-on-the-Lake in 1998 took the time to visit the Niagara Apothecary. They all noted the handsome gentleman wearing a dark suit and holding a cane who stood silently in the corner. He paid little attention to any of the people in the building. In fact, he seemed entirely engrossed with the various displays. At first, the family thought nothing of this man, assuming he was nothing more than a costumed re-enactor. They took a number of photos of the apothecary's interior, some of which included the silent man in the frame. They had no way of knowing these photos would cause them to question their views on life and death and the idea of the afterlife.

When the photos were developed sometime later, the family was shocked that the cane-carrying man was nowhere to be seen. They had expected him to be in three or four photos, yet he wasn't even in one. The only evidence that he had been there at all was found in a single image where a vaguely human-shaped, smoky aberration occupied the very spot where the gentleman had stood. The family debated the matter for a while, wondering if perhaps there was a logical explanation, but none presented itself. In the end they realized that they had seen, and partially photographed, an apparition.

One man, a self-described "sensitive" named Tim, had the most startling encounter with the ghost on record. It was fleeting, but terrifying. It was late one night; the streets were eerily empty. A tiny sliver of a moon winked down at him as he strode through the sleeping town. Passing by the Niagara Apothecary, Tim suddenly stopped and squinted at the building's large front window. He had heard what sounded like a soft, human sigh and sensed the presence of a figure within the darkened museum. The strength of the sensation made Tim curious—maybe even a bit reckless. He pressed his face up against the window of the apothecary, staring hard through the glass. Shadows draped over the perfectly preserved 19th-century interior, making details impossible to pick out. He suddenly jumped back in stark terror.

"Standing right on the other side of the window was a man with white curly hair wearing a formal black coat," Tim recalls. He was horrified, not only because of the figure's startling sudden appearance but also because the figure had no body below his shoulders. A blink of an eye later, the image was gone and Tim was alone in the empty street once more.

Pauline Raby, another psychic, investigated the Niagara Apothecary with paranormal researcher John Savoie for his book *Shadows of Niagara*. It's worth noting she knew nothing about the apothecary's history or legacy of hauntings before her arrival. Immediately upon entering the building, she sensed the presence of a warm and welcoming spirit. Like a moth to a flame, she was irresistibly drawn to the back of the building, where coincidentally most of the paranormal activity is described as occurring. Raby felt an unusual amount of spiritual energy concentrated there and concluded that the ghost residing in the apothecary is caring and compassionate, not malicious.

But who, exactly, is the resident ghost? That's a question that has perplexed many over the years. The one thing everyone, from psychics to eyewitnesses, seems to agree on is that it's a male figure with a palpable aura of authority—someone who is used to commanding respect from those in his presence. That description could easily apply to several prominent individuals connected to the Niagara Apothecary.

Judge Edward Clarke Campbell, whose practice operated out of this building for many years, is one candidate. He was a man used to getting his own way; after all, his word was, quite literally, the law in early Niagara-on-the-Lake. However, it's generally believed he already haunts the Old Courthouse, just across the street, where he presided as judge of the United Counties of Lincoln, Welland and Haldimand for decades.

Since many believe the ghost lingers because of the familiarity of his surroundings, which have literally deceived the spirit into believing time has stood still, it must be a pharmacist of yore. One possibility is Henry Paffard. In addition to owning and operating the pharmacy for some 30 years, he was also Niagara-on-the-Lake's longest serving mayor (a total of 23 years), in which capacity he wielded considerable power.

And then there was John De Witt Randall, Paffard's successor as village pharmacist. Randall was also mayor for one term, district deputy grand master of the Masonic lodge and a warden of St. Mark's Church. He was a beloved member of the community and exercised considerable influence over its affairs. Randall is the only one to die suddenly during his tenure as pharmacist. On March 12, 1914, he took ill unexpectedly and went home from the pharmacy early. He died a few short hours later of "paralysis of the brain," likely a stroke. Is John De Witt Randall the ghost who haunts the Niagara Apothecary? We'll likely never know for sure, but at least one psychic has come to believe it is indeed Randall.

Settled amidst the bloodshed of the War of 1812, Niagara is haunted by the ghosts of its violent and battle-ravaged past. You don't have to look far to find a museum, fortification, gallery, historic park or heritage homestead that is tinged by the presence of restless dead from this tragic period (some of them explored in my book *Ghost Stories of the War of 1812*, co-written by Maria Da Silva). And yet, somewhat ironically, one of the more haunted locations in the region, the Niagara Apothecary, has no ties whatsoever to this war-torn past. Indeed, the building is a reflection of a period of peace and prosperity. Here, within this thoroughly haunted building, a pharmacist remains on duty—a pharmacist who is taking dedication to one's job to unusual lengths. Visit this fascinating museum, step back in time and perhaps meet the pharmacist himself.

See For Yourself

The Niagara Apothecary is an excellent example of mid-Victorian commercial architecture. The original interior fittings of the apothecary, all in use for nearly a century from 1869 to

1964, have been painstakingly restored. The hub of the apothecary was the ornately carved dispensary, which dominates the rear of the main room. All manner of medications were made in the dispensary during its years of operation.

There are a number of unique artifacts on display that demonstrate just how far medical science has advanced since the apothecary first opened. The hands-down favourite is the glazed china leech jar. In the 19th century, leeches were sold to facilitate blood-letting therapies used for all manner of medical conditions. Then there is the enema box. Enemas were another popular treatment for all manner of ailments, but the enema box displays how uncomfortable such treatments would have been. The user basically sat and impaled himself on the ivory projection, then pushed down on the plunger at the front to force the necessary fluid up.

Other artifacts are less disturbing, including an early cash register and several ornate show globes, which hung in windows and were illuminated from behind to announce that medical assistance was available. The 1892 perfume dispenser is also of particular interest. Labelled "a scent for a cent," the customer inserted a one-cent coin into the slot, pulled the lever, and a mist of "the finest Paris perfume" sprayed out.

Ghosts or not, the Niagara Apothecary is an excellent place to visit.

Spectral Habits: Ghostly Nuns at Le Musée de Saint-Boniface Museum

~

No one who enters can deny that Le Musée de Saint-Boniface Museum lies within a time warp. Formerly known as Grey Nun's Convent, it houses one of Manitoba's finest collections of historic artifacts and is the oldest building in all of Winnipeg. It's also easily the city's most haunted building, thanks to a long and colourful past. When the glint of a moon casts dancing shadows upon earth, ghostly nuns walk amidst the rooms they inhabited in life, reminding us that while they may be gone, their blessings continue to protect this remarkable structure.

In 1844, the Grey Nuns, a Catholic order founded in Montréal and known for ministering to the poor and the sick sent four sisters to Manitoba to help with the education of girls in the West. The journey tested the mettle of these nuns; they covered 2900 kilometres in 58 days via canoe, portaging 150 times and enduring bitingly cold weather and dark clouds of mosquitoes. But they persevered, driven as much by their faith as by their physical strength. Upon arriving in Manitoba, the sisters quickly realized it wasn't merely education that the settlement lacked, but also care for orphaned children and medical attention in general.

The year after their arrival, construction of a convent in St. Boniface began. From this base, the nuns carried out missionary efforts throughout the West, spreading not just the word of God but also the comforts of civilization. Completed in 1847, the convent house served as western Canada's first hospital, orphanage and senior's home. It was also a school. Initially, both boys and girls were educated there (Louis Riel was a student), but eventually the sisters turned their attention to operating a girls-only boarding school.

In 1938, the sisters granted permission for La Société historique de Saint-Boniface (SHSB) to open a museum in the basement of St. Boniface Cathedral. The nuns couldn't have known then the important role the historical society would play in the eventual fate of the convent.

In 1956, the Grey Nuns tearfully vacated the building that had been their home for over a century. Rumours swirled about the future of the convent. Most people seemed to accept that the building would be demolished in due time. It was old, after all, and costly to maintain. The SHSB would hear none of this defeatist talk, however. They were determined to save it and, to that end, spearheaded efforts to have the convent designated a historic building for use as a museum. In November 1958, thanks to the tireless efforts of the historical society, the Historic Sites and Monuments Board of Canada designated the building a historic site and, as the SHSB had hoped, recommended that it be preserved for possible use as a museum. In November 1959, the City of St. Boniface took the lead on the project, created the Saint-Boniface Museum Board and began extensive renovations. Work was completed in 1967, in time for Canada's Centennial celebration.

The mandate of the Musée de Saint-Boniface Museum was, and remains, to safeguard the history and heritage of

French-Canadian and Metis people in Manitoba. The museum collects, preserves, researches and interprets artifacts of significance to French-Canadian and Metis people to further understanding of their contribution to the development of the Province of Manitoba. Among the extensive collection are such notable artifacts as Louis Riel's revolver and moccasins, a Red River cart in which people carried their worldly goods on the way to settling the Red River Colony, reminders of the fur trade in the form of a voyageur's sash and Hudson's Bay Company trade gun, and the mayor's chair from the former city of St. Boniface before it merged with Winnipeg.

Despite the fact that the Grey Nuns willingly vacated the building, it's believed that one or more of the sisters were so devoted to the convent and their charitable work there that they've remained behind in spirit if not in physical form. This explanation is the one given for much of the supernatural activity that enlivens the museum. Of course, the building served as both a hospital and a senior's home, so it's certain that numerous deaths would have taken place within these walls. It's quite possible that the spectral nuns share the museum with the spirits of some of the tragic souls they tended.

Unnatural sounds are frequently heard in the building. As one might expect of a building as old as this one, one will hear floorboards creaking underfoot, the foundation settling and pipes groaning and rattling. Employees are accustomed to such noises and pay them no heed. Even during dark evenings with the wind howling like a banshee outside and a storm threatening, the kind of nights when one's imagination might allow suppressed fears to emerge, long-serving staff members give such noises no second thought. But there are noises beyond these familiar sounds that cause staff to wonder just what secrets the building holds.

For example, footsteps are distinctly heard stalking the halls, and people have complained of mysterious, persistent rapping on walls. And then there's the giggling of a child at play. Staff will be working in the building after hours, long after any youthful guests have left, when they hear the joyful sound of a child's laughter echoing down empty hallways. Most of the time it's one child; other times it sounds like a little gang involved in hijinks. When you investigate, you can never find where the sounds are coming from. Just as you draw near and enter the room where you think the laughter was originating, the sound suddenly jumps to another room— almost as if the joke is on you.

A paranormal investigation team who spent an evening in the museum offered some potential insight. While they were no more successful than staff in pinpointing the source of the laughter, they apparently made contact with the spirit of a young boy who died there and, for unknown reasons, cannot find lasting peace. This child was unusually persistent after initial contact was made and kept trying to communicate with the group even after they told him they had to leave. Then after the ghost hunters had left for the night, the museum employee who had stayed behind to lock up found the ghostly lad to be still in a playful mood. She tried to turn on the alarm, a task she did routinely without incident, but it wouldn't set. She tried again— no luck. Indeed, it took four or five attempts before the employee successfully set the alarm. It seemed as if the boy didn't want to stop playing that night. Perhaps he is lonely in the afterlife.

Paranormal activity at Le Musée de Saint-Boniface Museum isn't limited to inexplicable noises. One year, the museum offered several opportunities for an authentic high-tea experience in an events room. Each one featured an elegant afternoon of Victorian charm, with tea cups and saucers set out on tables draped with white cloths; staff served tea and biscuits and finger sandwiches. This room, which previously had never been the site of spectral activity, suddenly came alive with unharnessed spiritual energy. All year long, chairs would be found scattered around the room and the cupboards would mysteriously fly open. The evening before high-tea events, staff would carefully set the tables by laying out the cups and saucers. It never failed: come morning the tea cups would be turned upside down. The staff was understandably annoyed at having to re-set the tables before guests arrived.

Months later, the annoyance receded a bit when it was learned who was turning the cups upside down and why. A visiting sister of the Grey Nuns explained that when tables were set in their dining rooms, cups were always placed upside down. Out of respect for the nuns who inhabited the building for its first century, employees began setting the tables in a like manner. After that, there was far less poltergeist activity.

One of the museum's exhibits depicts how the Grey Nuns lived during their century-long inhabitation of the building. This exhibit includes a bedroom, a living room and the dining hall. Among the furnishings in the bedroom is a rocking chair. Walking past the exhibit one day, an employee noticed the chair was rocking back and forth, creaking ever so slightly. The woman thought this was odd because there was nothing that could have caused the chair to rock—no air current, no vibration in the floor, no visitor who could have started it, nothing whatsoever. Nor did it slow, as gravity and friction dictate it must.

Back and forth, back and forth, it rocked endlessly. The woman began to imagine that an unseen nun was sitting in her former chair. With each rock she became more and more unnerved. Finally, she couldn't take the chair's unnatural behaviour any longer. She reached out with slightly shaking hands and stopped the rocking chair, then continued on with her work.

Not long after, she passed by the exhibit again and was startled by what she saw: the chair was rocking again. This time, the employee didn't have the courage to reach out and stop the chair. Instead she hurried on her way and put the chair with its invisible occupant behind her.

The spiritual echo of the Grey Nuns is often felt within the chapel. There you may hear gentle hymns being sung by female voices or catch the scent of roses or incense hanging in the air. On occasion, visitors have reported that they've felt someone tapping insistently on their shoulder, but when they turn around to see who's there, the chapel is eerily empty.

In the 1990s, prior to the renovations that added the gift shop and additional office space, the teller manning the front entrance could see all the way down the museum's hallway. One day, a female employee in conversation with the teller happened to look up and spot a human-shaped shadow prowling the hallway. She turned deathly pale as she watched it slink down the corridor, gliding silently along the wall and then out of sight. The employee's breath caught in her throat. She was terrified. When at last she could speak, she relayed what she had seen to the teller. Together, the two women decided to investigate to ensure the woman hadn't mistaken the unnatural shadow for that cast by another employee or visitor. There was no one to be found, which of course did nothing to calm the woman's racing heart. She was forced to concede that she had seen a shadowy phantom.

On another occasion, an employee walking past the downstairs washrooms heard the sound of water running in the women's washroom and dutifully went in to turn off the faucet. As soon as she entered, the door swung shut behind her. She shut off the water and went to leave, only to find that the door wouldn't open. Throwing her shoulder against the door did nothing; it wouldn't even budge. The woman fought down a rising tide of panic. Finally, whatever invisible force was imprisoning the woman in the washroom released its hold, allowing the employee to escape. A shiver ran down her back as she entered a hallway that was suddenly bone-numbingly cold, its lights flickering menacingly. The employee was left with the impression that she was in the presence of a malicious entity. Who might this have been in life? Surely not a member of the Grey Nuns, who dedicated their lives to caring for others. We may never know this dark spirit's identity, and maybe we shouldn't want to.

Le Musée de Saint-Boniface is a museum, yes, but it's also a holy place enriched with spiritual energy. Some of that energy comes from its past as a place of worship and charity, and some of it is of the ghostly kind, the result of souls that remain forever tied—whether by devotion or happenstance—to this unique building.

Whether you're interested in history or haunts, the museum is well worth a visit, though out of respect you may want to cross yourself before entering.

See For Yourself

Le Musée de Saint-Boniface Museum is recognized by the province as a Manitoba STAR Attraction, thanks in part to the heritage value of the building itself. Staff members like to point out that the former convent is in fact their principal artifact. It is the oldest remaining structure in the city of Winnipeg, the largest oak log building in North America, the first hospital in western Canada and a symbol of the 19th-century missionary effort carried out in the West by the Grey Nuns. The museum received a Heritage Canada Foundation award in recognition of the care taken to preserve historic integrity during the most recent round of renovations, from 1993 to 1995.

Also assisting in the museum being named a Manitoba STAR Attraction is its impressive collection and the engaging way in which it is interpreted for guests. Exhibits tell a comprehensive story of St. Boniface, from the First Nations who originally resided in the area through to the 20th-century city that merged with Winnipeg. The collection of First Nations artifacts is particularly impressive, including intricate beadwork (gloves, a coat and moccasins), a pestle used for pounding pemmican, a *tikinagan* or baby carrier, and archaeological specimens that include arrowheads, spearheads and stone tools. Representative of 19th-century European settlement are a variety of craftsmen's tools and early professional trappings (such as rather primitive-looking surgical instruments), items typically found in a pioneer home, agricultural implements and—in a nod to the Grey Nuns themselves—a range of religious objects. Exhibits are built around important themes such as the fur trade, the development of the Metis people, settlement of the Red River Colony, the Red River Rebellion and the evolution of the city of St. Boniface. There's even a fine arts collection that contains works by Franco-Manitoban and Metis artists.

Genealogists will find the Centre du Patrimoine (Heritage Centre) of particular interest. The more than 1300 photographs and hundreds of documents preserved here are a valuable resource to anyone interested in Franco-Manitoban and Métis history.

Roblin's Mill: Spiritual Heart of Black Creek Pioneer Village

~

Thousands of people visit Toronto's Black Creek Pioneer Village every year to experience what daily life was like for our pioneer ancestors. But it's possible the past is closer at hand than even the dedicated costumed re-enactors might realize because as many as a dozen of the 30-odd heritage buildings on site are haunted by the spirits of settlers. And when one stops to think about it, should it really come as a surprise that the museum is haunted? After all, Black Creek Pioneer Village is a monument to all those settlers who came to a young Canada and carved our nation from the wilderness. Their hopes and dreams, their trials and tribulations, their sweat and tears are tied to the buildings they left behind.

Long-dead horses are stabled restlessly within the confines of the Rose Blacksmith Shop. Sometimes they break free with frightful consequences. A grief-stricken woman gazes mournfully out from a window in the Burwick House, awaiting the return of loved ones cruelly snatched from her grasp. Sadly, her lonely vigil is doomed to be an eternal one. And in the cemetery, a young boy plays among the grey headstones, giggling mischievously when his sudden appearance startles onlookers. For details on these ghosts, please refer to *More Ontario Ghost Stories*, which I authored with Maria Da Silva.

In this chapter I share the shivers associated with Roblin's Mill, a gristmill almost 200 years old. The mill sits alongside a placid pond, its wheel creaking and rumbling as water spills over it and rotates it. Inside, the air is thick with the dry odour of grain. A thin layer of flour coats the machinery and floors, lending a ghostly aura to the cavernous interior. As would have been the case in any 19th-century community, the five-storey Roblin's Mill looms high over the other, more modest buildings in Black Creek Pioneer Village; it is an imposing and somehow romantic structure that captures the imagination of everyone who visits the living history museum. In a place where ghosts handily outnumber staff, it is perhaps appropriate that the towering mill is among the most haunted of the buildings comprising the museum. Roblin's Mill, then and now, is literally and figuratively—and yes, even spiritually—among the most important businesses in the community.

In the early 1800s, settlers harnessed the abounding water supply of rivers and streams throughout Ontario to power sawmills and gristmills. One of those entrepreneurs was 36-year-old Owen Roblin, the grandson of United Empire Loyalist Phillip Roblin. Owen built his gristmill in the Prince Edward County village of Ameliasburg, near Belleville.

An 18-metre-long canal, measuring 4.5 metres wide and 2.5 metres deep, was blasted from nearby Roblin Lake to the mill site. Water came through this canal, spilled 23 metres into the mill pond and then through a flume to turn a 9-metre-diameter overshot waterwheel. The spinning of this wheel turned three 2-metre millstones in the building, grinding grain into flour. The mill had a daily capacity of 100 barrels of flour. Horse-drawn wagons carried bags of wheat and rye flour to the docks in nearby Rednersville, where they were placed aboard ships for transport to Montréal, the United States, Britain and British colonies.

Like most mill owners of the era, Roblin thrived financially from his operation. In a short time, he was able to add extensively to the mill complex with a sawmill, carding mill and shingle mill, as well as a post office, bake shop and even a cooperage for the manufacture of barrels. The community thrived as well. Roblin's varied businesses provided jobs and valuable services for locals, especially the farmers who depended upon export markets for the wheat they grew.

In the decades after Roblin established his mill complex, the village developed rapidly so that by 1870 it had grown from just a handful of homes to include several general stores, a carriage shop, a harness shop, a couple of blacksmith shops, a large hotel and 300 inhabitants. Indeed, the mill was so central to the village's fortunes that the community was originally named Roblin's Mills.

The mill was at the height of its fortunes during the American Civil War of 1861–65, when demand for Canadian flour south of the border meant the mill literally worked around the clock. It was around this time that the ageing owner began to turn mill operations over to his eldest son, Edward.

Edward was fated to be the last Roblin to operate the mill. When he passed away in 1900 (three years before his father died at the age of 97, still serving as postmaster), a succession of owners came and went, each trying and failing to make the mill profitable at a time when the small-town mill was being eclipsed by industrial-scale urban mills. Operations ceased for good in 1920.

The building stood vacant for many years with most of its machinery still in place. Age took its toll. In the early 1960s, a serious crack developed in the masonry, and the mill's structural integrity was called into question. It began to look as though the mill would be demolished. Thankfully, it was saved from this unfortunate fate when it was purchased by Toronto's Black Creek Pioneer Village. In 1964, the mill was disassembled stone by stone, shipped to Toronto and rebuilt over the course of a year to provide visitors with an opportunity to see an early mill in full operation. Incredibly, the original timbers, flooring and machinery were all in sound condition and could be re-incorporated, making the mill truly authentic. The only real difference is the size of the mill wheel: it was determined that a 5.5-metre-diameter wheel could perform as efficiently as the original 9-metre wheel, so that change was made. Today, Roblin's Mill is the only operating stone gristmill in Toronto. Back at its original site, a plaque has been erected, and the millpond forms part of the Harry Smith Conservation Area.

Poet Al Purdy was a lifelong resident of Ameliasburg. As a boy, he grew up rambling in and among the eerie ruins of Roblin's Mill, and as an adult his youthful fascination was transformed into a deep respect for the history of this landmark. Purdy even made the mill the subject of at least one poem, simply entitled "Roblin's Mill," in which he seems to acknowledge encountering restless spirits during his childhood adventures in the building. In part, he wrote:

> *Those old ones you can hear them*
> *lost in the fourth dimension*
> *what happened still happens*
> *a lump rises in your throat.*

Roblin's Mill has been so faithfully restored at Black Creek Pioneer Village that even the spirits Purdy references made the trip from Ameliasburg. Seemingly trapped forever within the building's thick stone walls, they are as much a part of Roblin's Mill as the three huge millstones, the ancient timbers or the rattling machinery that modern visitors so admire.

Over the years since it found a new home at Black Creek Pioneer Village, many visitors and staff members have had unusual experiences at the historic mill, though none have been considered negative. A number of times, in the midst of winter, bundled up employees crunching through the snow-covered streets of the village have been startled to hear the creaking of the mill's waterwheel. *That can't be*, they think to themselves, *the waterwheel has been disconnected for the winter.* They stop in their tracks and listen carefully. Sure enough, the sound of the wheel is unmistakable. Hurrying through the streets, the employee invariably arrives at the mill to see the wheel somehow turning away as if going about the business of making flour.

One watchman recalls hearing the wheel turning one winter evening and shared his experience with me. "I was curious, and I admit a bit scared, because the wheel shouldn't have been able to work, so I headed over to the mill to check it out. When I got closer, the noise suddenly stopped. I arrived and stood staring off to the left where the mass of the wheel was outlined against the night sky. It was motionless," he explains. But that wasn't where the strangeness ended. "I heard the distinct sound of footsteps in the building, clomping heavily across floors. Of course, there was no one inside."

Cathy Carleton recalls visiting Black Creek Pioneer Village as a child in the 1980s. The mill, with its massive wheel and imposing stone walls, left a strong impression on her. "As we watched the huge wheel turning, I felt for a moment that we were living in olden days. The old wheel creaked as it turned.

But as we reached the steps to enter the building, the wheel suddenly stopped working," writes Carleton. She and her parents entered the building, looked around, snapped some photos and climbed to its highest floor to peer out at the village below. Cathy remembers racing through the building with youthful exuberance. "When we were leaving, we heard a creaking moan, and the wheel started to turn again. There was no miller in the building to start the wheel. It was really strange."

Maybe the mill wheel isn't turning away without purpose. Some people claim that spectres of the past continue the process of grinding grain into flour. Another verse from Purdy's poem eerily echoes the experiences of some visitors to the mill:

In the building men are still working
thru sunlight and starlight and moonlight
despite the black holes plunging down
on their way to the roots of the earth.

A spectral miller has been seen several times, hustling through the mill and disappearing into thin air. The ghost has even been captured in a photo taken by Catherine Crow, who led Halloween ghost tours at Black Creek Pioneer Village for a number of years. "The photo was taken on the night of the ghost walk in October 2007. There is a very distinct male shadow figure leaning against the door frame at the entrance to the mill. The door was open at the time," Crow explains. "It reminded me of an old worker from a different time taking a break from his work." Crow assures me there was no material being standing there at the time the photograph was taken.

What Crow couldn't possibly know is that I received a very similar eyewitness account recently. The claimant saw a shadowy figure casually standing in the very same doorway. After a second, it blurred with the shadows of the mill's interior; it was as if the apparition had stepped back inside to return to work. Perhaps the long-dead miller takes the occasional break from his eternal labour. After almost two centuries of hard work, who would argue he doesn't deserve it?

During another one of Crow's ghost tours, several members of a group taken into the mill claimed to hear the faint sound of singing coming from the lower level of the mill. Was this the sound of a mill hand singing to pass the time? Perhaps.

Robert and his family visited Black Creek Pioneer Village one Christmas for a festive feast in the Halfway House Hotel. It had snowed during the day, not much but enough to leave a thin, powdery cover over the ground. With Halloween almost two months past, ghosts were the furthest thing from Robert's mind when he and his family entered the village. That would change dramatic fashion just a few short hours later.

Pleasantly full after a traditional dinner of turkey, stuffing and cranberry sauce, Robert stepped out of the hotel and into the cold, pulling up his collar against the wind. He and his family decided to wander through the pioneer village for a while before returning to their cars. The windows of the village buildings were dark, staring blankly into the night. The night was eerily silent, save for the wind that occasionally howled through the trees and made the bare branches whip about.

Suddenly, the crisp winter air took on a creepy feeling and Robert heard the *clip-clop* of hooves coming nearer. A wagon drew into view, seemingly appearing out of the darkness itself. It creaked and rattled as it drove along the snow-covered street, heading in the direction of the silent mill. Robert followed, his shoes crunching over the patchy snow.

Robert watched in silent disbelief as the wagon drew up next to the mill and rolled to a stop before it grew faint, then disappeared entirely. He sucked in long, cold breaths, terrified. His eyes went to the snow-covered street at his feet. He saw his own footsteps behind him, but it was otherwise pristine, unmarred by the passage of a horse or wagon. Nothing of this earth had passed his way.

Interestingly, Robert's experience eerily echoes yet another verse from Purdy's poem, in which the poet seems to hint at ghostly wagons visiting the mill. He writes:

Old hands sift the dust that was flour
And the lumbering wagons return afloat
In their pillar of shadows
As the great wheel turns the world…

Catherine Crow offers up a final apparition that may be tied to the mill. "There is a ghost boy in 19th-century clothes who haunts the road in front of the mill leading down to the manse. He has been seen by employees and guests alike. He will appear for brief moments of time, play peek-a-boo and disappear again. He has also tugged on coats and other clothing of unsuspecting guests. He'll disappear by the mill and has not been seen past the mill," she explains.

Is this boy spiritually bound to the mill, or is his soul attached to the land itself? Is this ghost the same youth that plays mischievous games in the nearby cemetery? Who is he and how did he die? All questions for which we have no answers.

People have been whispering about ghosts inhabiting Roblin's Mill for nearly a century, beginning back when the building was a vacant and silent shell inhabited only by pigeons roosting in the rafters and vermin scuttling through the refuse. It is a measure of the strength of legends and tales—and of the strength of will of the inhabiting spirits—that they've endured for decades and followed the mill from Ameliasburg to its new location in Toronto hundreds of kilometres away.

Does a spectral miller still ply his trade? Does the mill wheel turn of its own accord under the dark cover of night? Visit Black Creek Pioneer Village and decide for yourself. Plan your trip for winter, when most of the experiences have been reported. Strain your ears. Is that merely the wind howling through the trees, or is it in fact the mill wheel groaning and creaking as it turns?

See For Yourself

Black Creek Pioneer Village is like walking onto a movie set in the past. Spanning more than 30 acres of rural landscape, the village is a living history experience filled with restored heritage homes, businesses and gardens that represent a typical crossroads community in southern Ontario during the 1800s. Visitors discover the joys and daily realities of living in early Ontario. Here at the village, the sights, sounds and smells are tangible reminders of our past. Meet the blacksmith, the tinsmith, the weaver, the miller, the printer and other people who bring our yesteryears to life.

With numerous events throughout the year, there's always something to do. Highlights include the Battle of Black Creek, a Revolutionary War re-enactment that includes 200 soldiers set up in camp; the longstanding Annual Pioneer Festival in September; Howling Hootenanny, a children's Halloween festival filled with pumpkin decorating, trick or treating, the haunted maze and other seasonal activities; and probably the highlight of the calendar, Christmas by Lamplight, a typical Victorian yuletide celebration.

The village is also home to Black Creek Historic Brewery. Visitors can participate in daily tours of an authentic 19th-century brewery, enjoy evening beer and cheese tastings and even serve as an apprentice for a day with the brew master.

A Spine-chilling Exploration of History at Haliburton House

~

S ome people need proof to believe in ghosts. I would direct such people to Haliburton House, the restored Windsor, Nova Scotia, home of celebrated Canadian author Thomas Chandler Haliburton. It's not so much that this atmospheric early 19th-century building has been the site of terrifying tales that will make your blood run cold—though there have been some of those over the years—but rather that you instinctively feel the presence of the dead there. It's palpable. History isn't some amorphous concept; it literally lives on in the form of restless spirits, Haliburton among them. When you're exploring the home or walking its grounds, you'll somehow know—a feeling deep down inside your core—that ghosts walk alongside you.

And why wouldn't this property be haunted? Haliburton House has seen a lot of history and human drama over the years. Some of it is celebrated by the costumed interpreters that staff the museum; some of it is only whispered about in hushed tones.

Naturally, the stories begin with the home's most famous resident, Thomas Chandler Haliburton. His apparition is the most commonly encountered by staff and guests. Let's travel together 200 years in the past to discover why he might remain attached to the home well after he should have slipped the bonds tying him to the realm of the living.

The son of a lawyer, judge and politician, Haliburton was born on December 17, 1796. As a young man, he became a lawyer and opened a practice in Annapolis Royal. It was the beginning of an auspicious career that saw him become a local judge, member of the legislative assembly for Annapolis County and justice of the Nova Scotia Supreme Court.

Haliburton wanted a home in keeping with his status. It also had to be large enough to accommodate not only himself and his wife, Louisa, but also a growing family that eventually included seven children. In 1833, he purchased an expansive estate and began construction of a fine house atop Ferry Hill, overlooking the town of Windsor, Nova Scotia. Construction wasn't completed until 1837, but all who saw it agreed it was worth the wait; the home was one of the finest in Nova Scotia at the time. A one-and-a-half storey centre wing with two-storey bedroom wings on either side, it reflected in both size and grandeur Haliburton's wealth and standing. Surrounded by lush gardens, fruit orchards, a pond and the fields and pastures of a working farm, the estate—dubbed Clifton, after Louisa's ancestral home in Britain—was an idyll for the Haliburton family.

It was here, at Clifton, that Haliburton secured a legacy for himself that endures to this day. Already the author of a number of books on such diverse subjects as history, politics and farm improvement, it was while living at Clifton that he wrote his most famous title, *The Clockmaker*, a humorous tale centred around the character Sam Slick. The book became one of the most popular of its era, and Haliburton became the first Canadian author to gain international recognition.

Sadly, Louisa passed away in the home in 1841 at the age of 48. Haliburton was heartbroken and for months was virtually inconsolable. Some say he never regained his previous vigour and passion for life. He remained at Clifton, but every day the familiar rooms and furnishings reminded him of his loss. Memories would bubble to the surface and old scars would burst into fresh wounds as his mind lingered on his dear Louisa. Eventually, perhaps unable to endure the torment any longer, Haliburton auctioned off the estate in 1856 and moved to England.

Here he finally found a measure of happiness again when he married Sarah Harriett Owen Williams. In 1859, he entered British politics and was elected a member of parliament. Thomas Chandler Haliburton's second lease on life was to be short-lived, however, as he suddenly grew sick and died in 1865.

Clifton, meanwhile, passed through a number of notable owners in the years after Haliburton sold it, some of who made additions and alterations that changed the home's original appearance. Among the more prominent owners were Senator Ezra Churchill of Hantsport; Daniel K. Hobart, a retired U.S. consul; W.H. Smith, a sea captain and hotelier; and Beckles Willson, a writer like Haliburton.

Despite the long and impressive list of owners over the years, by the early 1930s the house sat vacant. The years passed and it remained uninhabited. With no one to maintain the home and the grounds, Clifton began to weather and show its age. There was concern that it would fall into decay and that a historic structure would be lost, but thankfully, the government of Nova Scotia stepped in and purchased the property in March 1939. The official opening as a museum was the next summer: July 4, 1940.

Did Thomas Chandler Haliburton celebrate the opening of the museum alongside the gathered dignitaries and members of the public? Does he revel in the renewed interest in his life and work? Or does he resent the intrusion of gawking strangers into what he still considers his personal domain? It's impossible to know for sure, but what is certain is that he loves the estate so much that he returned to it in death. In the decades since the museum opened, his ghost has made its presence known many times and often in very dramatic fashion.

Picture this for a moment: you're in the reception hall of Haliburton House. There's nothing particularly wrong, yet something inexplicably feels off. Goosebumps prickle your skin and a cold sweat coats your back. Your senses are on high alert, like those of prey being hunted. You see nothing unusual, hear nothing untoward, but the pit in your stomach tells you something unnatural lurks near at hand.

Suddenly, there's an ominous groaning sound—aged wood and unoiled hinges. Spinning, you watch as a secret door on a nearby wall slowly swings open. Your stomach drops, the same feeling you get when the tracks suddenly drop out from under you on a roller coaster. You peer into the shadowy void behind the secret door, and then you see it. You step back. You want to cry out, but your mouth has suddenly become parched. You are literally paralyzed with fear.

Stepping out of the darkness is the ethereal form of a middle-aged man dressed in long-outdated garb. The apparition floats across the wooden floor with not so much as a creaking to mark his passage. As you stand there, rooted to the spot, the spirit advances toward you. Seconds creep by and you notice that his mouth is moving as if to speak, but no words come out of his mouth. The ghost is close to you now and slowly raises a hand above your head.

The sickening sensation of fear threatens to overwhelm you, but the spectral man passes by, paying you absolutely no mind—it's as if you don't even exist. His transparent hand, still raised overhead, waves at someone in the distance as he continues across the reception hall. You're still rooted to the spot when, moments later, the spectral figure simply vanishes from view.

Imagine how you'd feel witnessing this scene and how it would irrevocably alter your views on life and death and the hereafter. Many people don't have to imagine because they've lived every life-altering second of it (or a variation of it). Thomas Chandler Haliburton always appears from that same secret panel, always wanders across the reception hall and always ignores the startled witness. The only variation is in how the apparition vanishes. Sometimes he walks from the room and out of sight; sometimes he simply fades from view; and sometimes he returns to where he began his spectral walk and disappears back through the secret door.

Thomas isn't the only Haliburton still inhabiting the estate. His wife, Louisa, has been seen as well, though almost always in the gardens outside. This setting makes sense: she was an accomplished gardener and lovingly tended to the extensive orchards and flower gardens laid out around the estate. It was there that she was most happy, so it's to there that her ghost returns. She has been seen wandering the grounds, bent over a garden plot as if pulling weeds or even waving a ghostly farewell to departing visitors.

Elsewhere on the grounds, visitors come upon the dark, leaden waters of a notorious pool known as Piper's Pond. On many a morning, these waters are enveloped in a thick mist, lending them a sinister and ghostly air. At night, a dark spirit is said to emerge from the sullen water of Piper's Pond, his despairing cries discernible over even the wildest of gales that come in off the nearby ocean. He is the kilted ghost of a piper of the Black Watch Regiment. Some say that as his regiment marched through the Clifton estate on its way to Annapolis from Windsor, this unfortunate fellow fell in the pool and drowned. Others, pointing at the shallowness of the pond, suggest that he must have fallen victim to foul play to die in these waters (perhaps by hateful fellow soldiers, either forced under the surface or murdered and his body dumped there to hide the misdeed).

However he came to rest at the bottom of the pond, the spectre is doomed to eternal torment. Night after night he tries to escape the watery grave—some witnesses have seen him walking the grounds—but he always falters in his task and by morning finds himself floating motionless at the bottom of Piper's Pond. If you strain your ears, you may hear the faint sound of pipes filtering up from beneath the water's dark surface. Local legend says that if you run around the pond 20 times, the spectral soldier will rise up from the depths on a black, wild-eyed horse. However, no one knows why a piper would be astride a horse, leading to the tantalizing possibility that this tragic wraith is yet another lost soul haunting the grounds of Haliburton House.

"John" was visiting the Haliburton House Museum a few years ago when he had a frightening experience at Piper's Pond. John describes himself as a firm non-believer, or at least he did until that summer day changed everything. He was forced, in the most abrupt of ways, to accept the existence of ghosts as a result of what he saw.

"I was down by the pond when I noticed impressions made by a pair of boots in the grass. I followed the tracks with my eyes down to the water. The boot prints actually disappeared into the pond," John recalls. He walked closer to the water's edge and saw something beneath the surface a few feet out. He peered ahead, trying to make out what was in the water. Then the pond revealed its ghastly secret. John saw a human arm, naked and horribly white. His horror grew as an entire body came into focus.

"My first instinct was that someone had drowned in the pool, and I debated whether I was going to jump in or run for help. Then the body rose slowly toward the surface. It was a man, a soldier dressed in a really old-fashioned uniform. The body kept rising, coming slowly toward the surface," he continues. John was paralyzed with fear. He found himself staring deeply into empty holes where eyes had once been.

"The body bobbed to the surface and the jaw creaked open. I could literally hear it creaking, like an old screen door. I didn't wait around to hear what the thing said. I ran," John explains.

He had grown up with tales of the undead soldier stalking Piper's Pond. But although John was familiar with the tale, he had always taken it for little more than colourful folklore. He was completely unprepared for the terror that came with a paranormal encounter. And although he would willingly revisit Haliburton House (describing it as a great experience), he has no intention of ever wandering down to Piper's Pond again. The terror of that summer day may never entirely disappear, but John is far enough removed from it today to look back and have one regret: "I only wish I had been brave enough to stay long enough to see what the ghost was trying to say."

Ghosts can be found anywhere, but to my mind they belong to old ruined castles, windswept moors or stately homes like Haliburton House. Indeed, in Britain, any manor worth its name has a spectre or two that wanders its halls. Why should Canada be any different? I believe that spirits, wraiths, revenants, phantoms—call them what you will—return to places to which they bear a strong emotional connection. So it seems natural that old homes, weighed down with history and infused with the emotional life experiences of those who have inhabited them over the years, would be haunted by past residents. Maybe not every stately old home in Canada has ghosts in residence, but Haliburton House does—with some to spare.

See For Yourself

Wind your way up a tree-lined drive to the home of Thomas Chandler Haliburton, who lived in this handsome residence for 20 years. Here, you'll learn about Canada's first bestselling international author, a man whose relevance to history lies well beyond the written word (his work to inspire immigration to the wilds of central Ontario, for example, resulted in a county there being named in his honour).

Visitors are not just immersed in the life of this famous Nova Scotian, but also in the time period in which he lived; the mid-1800s come alive in the architecture, furnishings, décor and lifestyle on display at this living history museum. Haliburton House Museum is a designated historic property, valued as much for its gardens and surrounding grounds as for its unique Italianate villa-style construction and original interior elements.

"Tours are offered daily and are catered to the interest of the guests. We showcase the many interesting changes in the house and its owners over the last two centuries. For example, the house was partially burned at one point, and when you go up into the attic you can still see the burned timbers—history becomes tangible when you can see it," explains site manager Mike Huggins. "This house still has its secrets, and we're still learning things. I've heard stories of secret passages and hidden stairs. There's no evidence of it so far, but who knows?"

Haliburton House Museum hosts a number of special events throughout the year, including popular murder mystery evenings in autumn and Hidden Treasures, a behind-the-scenes tour featuring items guests don't normally see.

There's still more to this multi-faceted estate. "One wing of the historic home hosts the Windsor Hockey Heritage Museum. Our community was the birthplace of hockey, and the museum brings our rich hockey history to life through a number of exhibits," enthuses Huggins. "And our 27-acre property, which incorporates much of the former Clifton estate, including one-time farm fields and lush forests, is basically a town park."

An Ethereal Spirit at Newmarket's Elman W. Campbell Museum

~

Theres are few museums inhabiting old buildings that do not have some sort of strange story attached to them; the stories are as much a part of our heritage as the buildings themselves or the artifacts they contain. Ghost lore is a fascinating blend of local folklore and history, so it's appropriate that community museums such as Newmarket's Elman W. Campbell Museum have their share of ghostly tales to help illuminate history and the personalities from our past generations.

The Elman W. Campbell Museum traces its roots back to 1974, when the Newmarket Historical Committee was formed in the basement of the Newmarket Public Library with a mandate to collect and preserve Newmarket's 200-year history. By 1980, the committee had grown to over 100 members and outgrown the library basement, so the Town of Newmarket allowed the newly named Newmarket Historical Society to use the top floor of the old fire hall at 140 Main Street South both for their meetings and as a museum to house and display the many artifacts the society had collected over the years.

When it opened on June 26, 1982, the museum was staffed by dedicated volunteers from the historical society. In 1983, the museum had grown and developed to such a degree that the town hired a full-time curator, Elizabeth Sinyard.

In 1991, the museum moved to a new home in a former factory, at which time it was renamed the Elman W. Campbell

Museum in honour of the first chairman of the New-market Museum Board. Five years later, in 1996, the museum moved one final time, to the old North York Registry Office at 134 Main Street South, a building that is a historic artifact in its own right.

The North York Registry Office was built in 1884 as repository for land title records and registers of births, deaths and marriages in the area north of Toronto in the former County of York (now York Region). It was designed by architect John T. Stokes, who served as an engineer for the County of York and

The building that houses that the Elman W. Campbell Museum, a former Land Registry Office, is as much an artifact as any history item held within.

later went on to design a number of prominent buildings throughout Newmarket and Toronto. The building served in this role until 1980, when the records were moved to a new courthouse/registry office complex. It is the only remaining 19th-century registry office in York Region and is an architecturally significant structure, as reflective of Newmarket's history as the hundreds of artifacts on display within it.

One special relic from the past is rarely seen: a ghost lingers in an unearthly vault from which it emerges only occasionally to inadvertently chill staff and patrons. This soul does not sleep peacefully in the hallowed earth of a cemetery; the question is, why? Just who haunts the Elman W. Campbell Museum?

Although the museum has been in the North York Registry Office building since 1996, staff experienced nothing frightening, unexplained or even unusual for more than a decade. It wasn't until 2013 that strangeness began to take hold.

The first recorded encounter took place late one afternoon. It was about 4:30 PM, half an hour after the museum closed to the public and after everyone except for curator Elizabeth Sinyard had left for the evening. Sinyard was standing in the upstairs washroom with the door open when she froze for an instant. Had someone just walked past the washroom? She was certain she had seen a dark form glide past the door heading for the exhibit hall. The figure was too quick in its movements and too indistinct in its form to make out any specific details. It was just a dark, human-shaped shadow that made absolutely no noise as it passed. Nonetheless, Sinyard was certain she had seen *something*. In fact, she was so convinced someone had walked—or, perhaps more appropriately, floated—past the door that she slowly, cautiously, poked her head out of the washroom to investigate. She was relieved to find that there was no one there, nor anywhere else in the building, but what remained was a lingering question: does a phantom haunt her museum?

A while later, one of the museum volunteers had an experience all his own. This individual is sensitive to spirits. He can feel their presence, sense their emotions, "hear" their thoughts and often gain an impression of who they were in life. One afternoon he was standing in Sinyard's office doorway when he said, matter-of-factly, "Oh, the ghost just walked by." Intrigued, Sinyard pressed him for details.

According to this man, the ghostly figure is male, wears a grey suit and walks a familiar route through the museum. His manifestations begin in front of a display honouring early New-market settler William Roe, where he's seated facing the recreated 1850s parlour as if at an unseen desk. He then stands, turns around, walks briskly in an arc by the washroom door and then down the hallway before disappearing into the museum vault where artifacts not on exhibit are stored. He unfailingly takes the exact same route, never deviating, his movements locked into some sort of eternal loop as if he is destined to recreate this walk for eternity.

Sinyard was struck by the extraordinary details provided by the volunteer and took it upon herself to dig into the validity of his claims. Did the historical record match the psychic volunteer's impressions? To her surprise, it seemed to. She discovered that, in the years before the building became a museum, there was a reception desk outside the present washroom and in front of the Roe exhibit—just as the sensitive seemed to indicate. This could explain the arc the spirit takes in his wanderings; in death he continues walking a familiar route, which includes stepping around a desk that stood on that spot in his time.

Furthermore, Sinyard's inquiries may have discovered the identity of the ghost himself. "There used to be an employee of the registry office who had a brisk walk and dressed conservatively in grey and navy, and who came to a tragic ending— though not, thankfully, in this building," she explains, noting that this description matches the appearance and behaviour of the museum's ghost as described to her. She also notes that the volunteer who described the spirit's distinctive route didn't know about the employee or the reception desk. Although Sinyard believes she knows the ghost's identity, she refuses to share it: "We will not name the former employee because it is recent history, out of respect for any living relative," she explains.

The next paranormal experience took place on March 12, 2014, at about 9:45 AM. The museum's volunteer registrar was coming out of the multi-purpose room when she thought she saw a man in a grey jacket walk briskly past the double doors toward the hall. She and two other staff members searched the building top to bottom, concerned that someone may have somehow slipped in undetected. No one could be found, and in retrospect it doesn't seem possible for a flesh-and-blood visitor to have entered the building unknown because there is a buzzer on the exterior doors that activates whenever they are opened. With no logical explanation, all agreed that the man in the grey suit was not of this world. The registrar was unnerved; her hands shook so much that she couldn't type afterward.

During 2015, the Elman W. Campbell had a Steampunk display with exhibits incorporating technology and aesthetic designs inspired by 19th-century industrial steam-powered

machinery. With the popularity of this subgenre of science fiction and science fantasy, it should come as no surprise that the
exhibit was well received. But perhaps not everyone was
impressed; the appeal of Steampunk may not extend to the dead.

One morning, a pith helmet that rested securely on a
mannequin in the Steampunk display was found on the floor
several feet away. "It could not have fallen or rolled there on its
own. We try to supervise all visitors and were not aware of anyone climbing into the display. It seems odd that if someone tried
it on for a lark they would have placed it on the floor instead of
back on the mannequin. This episode is merely strange and may
mean nothing at all," explains Sinyard.

But later that year, Sinyard was away at an outreach
event and her curatorial assistant was staffing the museum until
3:00 PM. The assistant was alone in the building when she heard
the sound of doors slamming at the back of the building. She
went to check that there was no one else in the building and
came up empty in her search. She was indeed alone. Although
that knowledge reassured her, it also left her a bit shaken because
it meant that unearthly hands had opened and shut the doors.

Sinyard had the same experience five days later. It was
nearly 6:00 PM, hours after the museum had closed to the public,
and everyone else had just left for the night. She was in her office
gathering up her belongings when she heard a door slam at the
back of the museum. It sounded like an office door, but there is
no door of that kind back there. A shiver crawled up her spine.
The thought of being alone in the building with a restless spirit
as dusk approached froze her blood. Never before uneasy in the
museum she had managed for two decades, the curator was suddenly terrified and ran from the building as quickly as possible.

Ghost stories are, quite naturally, associated with Halloween. It's believed by some that at this time of year the veil between the realms of the living and dead becomes thinner and that spirits of the deceased are able to more freely enter our world. Many locations reputed to be haunted report a significant increase in the number and intensity of paranormal phenomena every October. Based on the following stories, the Elman W. Campbell Museum is no different.

Just before Halloween 2015, a museum volunteer purchased and donated a life-size witch mannequin to add some spooky atmosphere to the building. The crone-like witch is activated by motion sensors. When someone draws near, her eyes suddenly glow an intense, fiery red and she speaks in a croak. She is, in a word, chilling.

The witch was installed in the exhibit next to the archives. Several times she awoke for no reason, her eyes suddenly glowing red, her cackle echoing in an empty exhibit hall. Most often, she sprang to life when someone was exiting the washroom, which was too far from the figure for the motion detectors to be activated by the movement. Sinyard tested the distance to be sure; the washrooms were just too far away. Looking for a rational explanation, she considered whether there might be a slight power surge caused by the automated door and light switch in the washroom. She tested her idea a few times, but it never worked. Even walking right past the figure to unplug her power cord at the end of the day wasn't enough to turn her on.

So if human movement wasn't responsible, what then was rousing the witch? Staff came to believe it was the passing of the resident ghost as he wandered the building. The site where the witch stood was on the route the ghost was said to walk on his tour of the museum.

It isn't just staff members who feel the chilly touch of the paranormal in the Elman W. Campbell Museum. Once, a boy of about 12 years old came in the side door with his family. He took one tentative step into the gallery and refused to go any farther, saying the museum was haunted. Genuinely scared, he couldn't be compelled or coaxed to enter; no amount of reassuring by his parents made the slightest dent in his conviction. And so the family left.

Within the museum are a number of exhibits that immerse visitors in Newmarket's rich past. A mysterious ghost wanders among them.

Then there was the experience of Henrietta, a Newmarket resident who reached out to me via email with a chilling tale. She had visited the museum in late autumn 2016. It was an enjoyable afternoon spent exploring the history of the town she had only recently moved to. She was particularly struck by the 1920s kitchen and how it looked like something straight out of a Norman Rockwell painting.

Henrietta was heading to the doors and was only steps away from being out in the brisk autumn weather when the sudden rise of a moaning wind sounded in the entryway. The door stood firmly shut, but Henrietta was chilled. Then she began to hear faint whispers all around her. The moaning came not from the wind but from the dead. She was convinced that spirits attached to some of the artifacts in the museum didn't want her to leave. Although startled, she politely told the dead that she had to leave but that she had enjoyed her time at the museum and wished them peace. The whispering suddenly stopped; the mysterious chill lifted, and Henrietta felt it was safe to leave.

It is pleasant enough to visit a community museum, especially one as immersive and well-designed as the Elman W. Campbell, and there reflect on the lives of those who have inhabited the town through the ages. If you know there is a possibility of actually meeting an ethereal figure from the past, the outing has added excitement.

Staff at the Elman W. Campbell Museum generally accept that their building is haunted by a former employee of the North York Registry Office. Is he lingering out of eternal devotion to his former job? Or maybe he remains to check up on the unique historical collection that is now displayed in his former workplace, a collection that represents a valuable window into the history of the community he dedicated his life to serving.

See For Yourself

The Elman W. Campbell Museum captures the diverse history of Newmarket, from its roots as a Quaker settlement in the early 1800s, through its period as a thriving market and industrial community in the mid-19th century and on to its present as a modern, cosmopolitan city.

Hundreds of diverse artifacts have a story to tell. There's a lock from a mysterious early 19th-century jail that exists only in oral history; an 1880s lantern from the original Congregational Church, one of the first "electrified" buildings in town, which burned to the ground in 1896—ironically, the result of faulty wiring; a book from the Mechanic's Institute, the forerunner of the modern-day public library system; and a somewhat perplexing town seal, which unlike the current town seal with its nine bees in a hive of activity inexplicably depicts only five bees hovering around the hive.

The exhibit halls are engaging and immersive. A circa-1850s living room reflects the life and times of William Roe, fur-trader, merchant and Newmarket founding father, while a 1930s office not only opens a window into white collar working conditions of a century ago but also honours one of the community's leading businesses, Office Specialty Co. And an eerily authentic World War I trench, complete with a contemplative soldier thinking of his home and loved ones far away, transports us to northern France during that conflict.

If you get the chance, a visit to this museum is well worthwhile.

~

Damned Souls Haunt Fort Calgary's Deane House

~

Nat remembers the first time she heard about the ghosts of Fort Calgary's Deane House. She and Maureen, her girlfriend and fellow ghost hunter, were speaking with an elderly man about the dark folklore surrounding the building.

The old-timer looked at them with black, bead-like eyes. "Been so long that I disremember the dates, but plenty of folks have died strange deaths within those walls. They were before my time, but I heard the elders tell about it," he said as he leaned back against a porch railing. He knocked ash from his pipe with the heel of his gnarled hand. "Some of them were bad seeds, so when they died Heaven wouldn't take 'em, and neither did Hell. Yessir, they came back and haunt the building to this day."

Nat and Maureen had hung on every word as the old man, his black eyes now gleaming with excitement, dove enthusiastically into the tale. He told of suicides and murders and those who refuse to truly die. But back in the safety of their home, the couple concluded that the old man's stories were nothing more than colourful yarns intended to entertain and frighten his captive audience. After all, no building could be *that* tainted with horror—could it?

A few week weeks later, spurred by the old timer's chilling stories, the women decided to investigate the location for themselves. What followed was a moment of terror Nat will never forget. It started around 2:00 AM when Nat, alone in front of the Deane House, found herself growing uneasy in the darkness.

"Mo! Mo!" As she called, Nat's voice was a tight whisper. She wanted desperately for her girlfriend to return to her side, yet somehow hated to break the hush of that October night. Maureen was somewhere behind the Deane House, taking electronic voice phenomena (EVP) readings of a building whose history they had learned was soaked in blood, tragedy and tales of the supernatural.

Finally, Nat couldn't take the fear any longer and headed off in search of Maureen. Rounding the building, she saw the other woman standing oddly erect with her arms limp at her sides and the EVP monitor lying in the dew-soaked grass at her feet. Her eyes were focused on a spot on the ground directly below a second-storey window. Maureen was rocking back and forth and mumbling as if carrying on a conversation with someone. She appeared to be in some kind of trance. Nat called her name, but Maureen showed no sign of hearing her.

Nat was terrified. Her heart raced and she was trembling. She cautiously approached Maureen and reached out a shaking hand to touch her. There was no reaction. Nat finally grabbed hold of her girlfriend's shoulders and shook her hard, desperately calling her name as she did so. Finally, Maureen's eyes flickered and there was a hint of recognition in them. Still, she seemed dazed and confused, so Nat took her by the hand and led her back to their car, then home.

Maureen slowly began to shake off the effects of whatever had overwhelmed her back at the Deane House (Nat refers to it as "sobering up") and explained that she had been having a conversation with a woman who had jumped from the second-storey window. But as often happens when you wake from a dream, details of what was said began to fade as soon as Nat pulled her from the trance. Maybe, they were now forced to admit, there was more truth than fiction in that old man's yarns. Maybe the Deane House was as filled with horror as they had been led to believe. Maybe the Deane House comes by its haunted reputation, which has seen it written up in newspapers, magazine and books, honestly.

The Deane House sits on the grounds of Fort Calgary National Historic Site, the birthplace of the city of Calgary. In the summer of 1874, 150 men of the North-West Mounted Police marched west across the prairie from Manitoba to establish a series of forts that would assert Canadian sovereignty and bring law, order and civilization to Canada's untamed western territory. Fort Calgary was built in 1875, and a settlement sprang up in the shadow of its palisade that, over the next quarter-century, grew into a thriving community. Fort Calgary served as a police headquarters, hospital and social centre for young Calgary, and it was a focal point for settlers, ranchers and businessmen in the region.

In 1914, the now Royal North-West Mounted Police (RNWMP) abandoned Fort Calgary and sold it to the Grand Trunk Pacific Railway. For the next six decades, Calgary's origins were hidden under a railway yard and storage area. In 1974, the City of Calgary bought the site and returned the city's birthplace to the public domain.

Undoubtedly, the most spiritually active building in Fort Calgary is the Deane House. Haunted by its troubled

past, the Deane House has chased away more people screaming in terror than perhaps any building in the entire province
(if you ask local paranormal researchers, they will without
hesitation tell you Deane House deserves to hold the bragging
rights—if such things are worth boasting of—to the title
"Alberta's Most Haunted Place"). To say its reputation is sinister is something of an understatement, which is a shame considering its historic value and the charm of the restaurant that
today occupies the building.

The Deane House was built in 1906 as the official residence for RNWMP superintendent Richard Burton Deane, his
wife and their five children. It never became the lively and happy
family home envisioned. Mrs. Deane died that year before ever
stepping foot in the house, and Deane shipped his children off
to be cared for by relatives. Instead of a home alive with youthful energy, the Deane House became somber and cold as the
mourning superintendant took up a lonely residence there.

When the RNWMP left Fort Calgary in 1914, the
Grand Trunk Pacific Railway moved the house a short distance
away for use as the station master's home. In 1929, the Deane
House was moved again, this time to its present site across the
Elbow River. The new owner, C.L. Jacque, made extensive alterations while transforming the house into a seedy boarding house
known as Gaspe Lodge. It remained a boarding house for four
decades, and with each passing year the once-grand RNWMP
residence was soiled deeper and deeper. Inside, the wallpaper
was water stained and peeling, black mould spots dotted the
ceilings and the floorboards were warped and splintering.
Respectable people gave it a wide berth.

During these years, the house was the site of an unusual number of deaths, many of them violent and gruesome, some of them mysterious. In the 1920s, a man was pushed down the stairs. When his body finally came to rest at the base of the staircase, he was dead—his neck broken, his body a bloody mess. And that was just the beginning of the Deane House's grim tally. After that horrifying incident, a young woman committed suicide by jumping from one of the upper windows; a prostitute was wounded in grisly fashion and left to bleed out on the wooden floorboards; and man was gunned down on the front porch. The tragedy that captured the most headlines, however, was when a husband strangled his wife before the eyes of their children, then said goodbye to his little ones and shot himself dead. That's a lot of death for one building.

When the City of Calgary bought the now-decrepit boarding house as part of the Fort Calgary purchase in 1974, they restored it to resemble what it would have originally looked like when built for Superintendent Deane back in 1906. Designated a National Historic Site alongside the rest of Fort Calgary, part of the building became a museum and another part a restaurant. Staff members soon became accustomed to uncanny happenings and ghostly appearances that sometimes, according to reports, were surrounded by a halo of light.

Haunting noises frequently sent chills down the spines of staff and guests alike. An antique telephone sits on Deane's desk in the study. Although it looks authentic, the phone is only ornamental. Despite this, the telephone occasionally rang. Spectral footsteps paced across floors and descended the stairs, and laughter would echo out from the front foyer. When staff would investigate these sounds, there was never an explanation that satisfied rational minds.

But spooky goings-on were not limited to inexplicable noises. Deane's study is furnished to reflect how it might have looked in the early part of the 20th century—hence the old-fashioned telephone—when the superintendent would have conducted business at his desk or perhaps read a newspaper in a comfortable chair at the end of the day. It's entirely appropriate, then, that the ever-so-slightly ethereal ghost of a man was frequently seen sitting in the cushioned chair. He never paid any heed to anyone and perhaps never even knew his privacy was being intruded upon. Instead he simply sat there, smoking his pipe, staring off into oblivion. Many people believe this spirit was Deane himself, reliving lonely evenings of yesteryear when he mourned the loss of his wife and the absence of his children.

Others, however, point to another possibility. During its years as a boarding house, an elderly man passed away of natural causes while sitting in a chair in this room, simply closing his eyes one night and never awakening. It has been suggested that the spirit might well be that of this poor man, rather than the RNWMP officer.

Many staff members refused to venture up into the attic. A strange stillness hangs over this shadow-filled room, and the atmosphere is eerie enough to elicit cold shivers. The walls and floors, un-renovated and largely as they were when built a century ago, radiate a feeling of melancholy. Perhaps that mysterious red stain soaked so deeply into the grain of the floorboards that it resists every effort to remove it is responsible. Perhaps it's also responsible for the nebulous wraith reported up there on numerous occasions—and still to this day.

In years past, the Deane House hosted much-anticipated murder-mystery dinners. Actors would portray their roles while interacting with the guests and then commit a "murder" that the participants would be tasked with solving before the evening ended. The entire building was essentially one large crime scene that the guests were free to explore. Only one area was explicitly off limits: the basement. One evening, a woman decided to ignore the rule. She descended the stairs to check out the basement. A while later she returned, steaming mad. The woman confronted a staff member to vent her anger. She explained that an old Native woman with long braids told her, much too sternly for her liking, that she should not be in the basement. She thought the woman—who she assumed was a costumed staff member—should have been more polite. The staff member calmly explained that there was no Native woman on staff that evening, then raced downstairs to investigate for herself. She found no one and was left with only one conclusion: the guest had encountered the spirit of a woman from one of the Native tribes that camped there in centuries past.

Once, a staff member watched in horror as man whose body seemed to disappear at the knees floated silently down the stairs towards him. The apparition wasn't ethereal; it could have been mistaken for a flesh-and-blood person if not for the abrupt manner in which the figure simply faded away at mid-leg. The ghost was dressed in a black cloak and hat in a fashion that looked to be from the 1920s and appeared to be middle-aged. It descended the stairs, crossed the foyer and then exited through the front door. Even though it had passed within a few feet of the stunned waiter, the ghost paid him no mind.

Atez Jacki was a long-time employee of the Deane House. At first the paranormal activity caused him sleepless nights as he tried to reconcile what he thought he knew about life and death with what he was experiencing first hand. Slowly, however, he became accustomed to the presence of the ghosts to the point where he rarely gave them much thought. Even when the ghosts made one of their occasional appearances, the waiter was generally unperturbed—but not always. There was one time when Atez fled from the Deane House in abject terror.

It was the summer of 1990, and he was alone in the building when he heard footsteps coming down the staircase. They were extremely heavy and purposeful, like the plodding steps of a stalker from a slasher movie. Atez was horrified. He was sure someone, or something, was coming to get him. With each step he heard, he felt certain his doom was that much closer at hand. Atez dropped what he was doing and raced from the building, pausing only long enough to turn on the motion detectors. In the yard he struggled to catch his breath and calm his frayed nerves. It was many minutes before he felt his pulse slowing and his ragged breath returning to normal. When at last Atez built up the courage to re-enter the building, he tentatively stepped inside, unsure of what he would find. He felt reassured when he noted the motion detectors hadn't registered anything; clearly there wasn't an intruder. But Atez couldn't dismiss the feeling of impending doom that he had felt. Was the ghost intent on doing him harm? Thankfully, as he pressed on, the waiter noted that the oppressive feeling had lifted. He no longer felt threatened.

It seemed that with each passing year, ghostly activity at the Deane House was growing more intense and more prevalent. Concerned that it was reaching some unknown creepy crescendo, in April 1990 it was decided to exorcise the historic building of whatever past transgressions were polluting its energy. The day after the exorcism was a particularly unsettling one for staff. Electrical appliances started and stopped working for no reason, clocks read the wrong time, items slid across countertops on their own and cutlery rattled on tables. The atmosphere was electric. Some staff members were so frightened they were unable to continue their shifts and left early. Everyone involved was concerned that the exorcism had the opposite effect of what was intended, riling rather than soothing the spirits. By day two, however, things had settled considerably, and since then ghostly activity has been greatly reduced. The exorcism seems to have worked. Only the attic, with its sinister red-stained floor, remains spiritually active today.

No one is certain of the identity of these ghosts whose shades were seen all over the historic Deane House and who were responsible for all manner of strange phenomena. No one is even certain if these spirits are truly gone or if they have simply recessed farther into the shadow-filled gaps between the floorboards or behind the walls. Have they finally found some lasting peace, or are they doomed to remain on earth because, as that gnarled old man told Nat and Maureen, neither Heaven nor Hell will accept their souls?

See For Yourself

Located a mere 10-minute walk from downtown Calgary, Fort Calgary encompasses a number of attractions beyond the Deane House, spread out over a 16-hectare park. A reconstructed 19th-century barracks houses an interpretive centre with museum exhibits telling the history of Calgary's first century (1875–1975), including the pivotal role of the NWMP and Fort Calgary in founding the community. Within the interpretive centre are replica rooms of many important historical structures from the city's past, including the original Canadian Pacific Railway station from 1883, the NWMP barracks from 1888 and the *Calgary Herald* newspaper composing room from 1932. Other exhibits in the museum bring to life prominent figures from Calgary's past.

Elsewhere on the grounds is Hunt House, the oldest building in Calgary in its original position. Built in 1876 as part of the Hudson's Bay Trading Post, it was newly restored in 2015 and designated a Provincial Historic Resource. Nearby, a community garden harkens back to the North-West Mounted Police garden, which was tended by Mounties and prisoners to provide fresh produce for the garrison. The modern garden grows and distributes produce to local charities and demonstrates ecological gardening techniques.

Ask about interpretive tours, which can range from a 20-minute presentation about Fort Calgary's history in the interpretive centre's theatre to a one-and-a-half-hour guided tour through the entire site and its buildings.

Ghost Town:
Muskoka Heritage Place

~

The sun settles below the horizon and shadows stretch across the forested landscape, shrouding the historic buildings of this recreated pioneer village in menacing darkness. Somewhere off in the distance a coyote howls mournfully, its cries the only sound to break the unnatural stillness of the night. You shiver almost uncontrollably, both from the chill and from the growing certainty that one of the spirits inhabiting the pioneer village is stretching out an ethereal arm in greeting.

Welcome to Muskoka Heritage Place after dark. The premier museum in Muskoka, with almost two dozen 19th-century buildings and an extensive collection of artifacts displayed in an award-winning exhibit gallery, is the site of countless stories of restless wraiths and playful poltergeists. Many staff members over the years have been wary of being alone while closing certain buildings once dusk begins to settle upon the village. They hurry to lock up the buildings, knowing that to take too long is to risk a meeting with one of the spectral inhabitants that have lingered well past their allotted time on earth.

Most visitors experience Muskoka Heritage Place under the glorious warmth of a Cottage Country summer sun, but it isn't necessarily a guarantee that they won't have a paranormal encounter. Whether it be in the Spence Inn, the charming home of Reverend Hill, the soot-filled blacksmith shop or the mysterious Orange Lodge, phantoms make their presence felt, serving as ethereal reminders of Muskoka's sad and occasionally dark past.

Spence Inn: Halfway to Heaven...or Hell

The Spence Inn is easily the largest building at Muskoka Heritage Place. Its size, the wrap-around porch and the grandeur of its furnishings instantly indicate this was a building of importance. But what isn't immediately apparent to visitors is the fact that this building is probably the most mysterious location at the recreated pioneer village, and that contained within its grey walls are ghosts and whispered legends of foul misdeeds. Countless people stayed there during its time as a roadside inn—perhaps more came than went.

The inn was built in 1878 by 54-year-old Sevitt Simpson, who had just stepped off the boat from his native England. With his wife, Ann, and four children in tow, he headed for the wilds of Parry Sound District and took up a new life as a hotelier in the hamlet of Spence. Sitting alongside the Nipissing Road, which ran from the village of Rosseau in the south to Lake Nipissing in the north, the inn catered to road-weary travellers. Because it was located roughly at the road's midway point, Simpson named his establishment the Halfway House.

At the time, Spence was a thriving little community with two stores, a blacksmith, two sawmills, a church, a school and about a dozen log homes. Most of the inhabitants were farmers, but the soil was too thin to provide for anything beyond subsistence-level agriculture. They and the village they founded were sustained by logging and serving the needs of travellers passing along the Nipissing Road. As long as those industries endured, so too would this hamlet.

Unfortunately, both road travellers and logging were fated to fade rather quickly. By 1896, a railway had been completed to

North Bay, causing traffic along the Nipissing Road to decline rapidly. And by that time, the forests in the region had been denuded of their harvestable timber, causing lumber companies to pull up stakes and move farther north. Settlers followed suit, abandoning failing bush farms for greener pastures. These events spelled doom for the Halfway House. The once-bustling business began to change hands every few years, and with each sale, its clientele and value decreased. Finally, it closed for good in 1911 and was purchased for use as a home by Hamilton Brown, a local school teacher who retired and took up farming. From that point on, the building served as a private residence.

By the 1950s, the home's final resident, William Thomas Doherty, had passed on and the entire community was enveloped in a ghostly shroud. No more than two homes were lived in; and the hamlet had been reduced to a handful of weathered and leaning buildings, crumbling foundations and empty cellar

A number of ghostly guests refuse to check out of the historic Spence Inn.

holes. The owners of the former hotel simply abandoned it, walking away from the malaise that seemed to cover the area. Decades passed and the inn decayed. Sad and neglected, it was close to ruin when, in 1977, it was moved to Muskoka Heritage Place, where it was painstakingly and accurately restored and renamed the Spence Inn.

Today, as costumed innkeepers guide visitors through the rooms and the realities of 19th-century hotels, sometimes the spirits of former innkeepers and tenants walk across the worn floorboards beside them, having followed the building from the northern hamlet it once called home to the recreated pioneer village. No one knows for certain who the ghosts inhabiting the Spence Inn were in life, but there are stories that offer suggestions. The tales surrounding the inn have grown taller with the passing years, but somewhere in these stories likely exists some element of tragic truth.

One story suggests that the ghost is a travelling doctor, an incompetent and uncaring physician who left a path of misdeeds in his wake. This man was more charlatan than healer, selling fake medicines, offering patients false diagnoses, botching even relatively simple procedures such as delivering babies or setting bones, and offering baseless advice. He preyed upon his patients, abusing their trust with his position. Guilt causes the doctor to return to the Spence Inn, the site of so many of his grievous deeds. Here he languishes, the former hotel now a prison for his soul.

One of the rooms in which unusual phenomena most frequently occur is located on the upper floor, a room furnished as a doctor's office. There's an old wheelchair, shelves lined with medicine bottles, a desk littered with 19th-century stethoscopes and other early tools of the trade, and textbooks on human anatomy and the latest medical practices. The room reveals an important role played by early inns: that of an office for dentists, salesmen or, in this case, doctors. These professionals would often travel around the area, providing services to the innkeeper and his family in exchange for room and board. In this manner, small rural communities would gain the benefit of medical and dental services that they otherwise would have gone without.

This room, indeed the entire second floor, is marred by an unpleasant spiritual presence that lingers to this day. Like a deep stain, this dark taint—the product of foul deeds gone unpunished—can't be removed, no matter how many years pass and how much the building has changed over time.

There is another, even more scandalous story surrounding the Spence Inn that might help explain its long history of hauntings. According to legend and whispered innuendo, a vagabond arrived at the inn one day, exhausted from his wanderings, starving, his clothes little more than rags that hung from his painfully thin body. The innkeeper and his family took pity on him, seeing the man beneath the savage.

Days turned into weeks, and the vagabond remained at the inn. He did odd chores to pay for his room and board and slowly became an accepted member of the family. The innkeeper was so consumed with his work and achieving the elusive goal of prosperity that he didn't see the budding attraction between his wife and the man he had welcomed into his home.

One day, the innkeeper disappeared suddenly and without a trace. His wife, with a well-rehearsed tale and equally well-rehearsed tears, sobbed that he had up and left her and their children, simply abandoning them in the middle of the night. She played the role of the wronged wife to the hilt, appearing hurt and vulnerable to her neighbours. No one suspected that this poor woman was anything but what she appeared.

A few months later, the vagabond slid into the position of both innkeeper and family man. There may have been some whispers in town that the relationship developed too quickly by the standards of the day, but most friends and neighbours were just pleased to see that the woman would be taken care of and that her tears had given way to radiant smiles. Soon, no one gave any thought to the relationship. It looked as if the matter was closed.

A couple years later, however, someone approached the young daughter of the innkeeper and inquired where her father was. It was an innocent question, but the answer rocked the community. "There," the young girl said sweetly as she pointed to the ground beside the inn. Word of the shocking revelation spread, and people began to question just what had occurred behind the closed doors of the inn. Had the innkeeper abandoned his family as everyone was led to believe, or did he lie in a shallow grave right under their noses? They had to know the truth. The area pinpointed by the girl was dug up and, sure enough, a rotting body was discovered.

Folklore doesn't tell us what befell the vagabond and his lover. We can't even say for certain how much of the story—if any at all—is real. The line between fact and fiction can be a hazy one, and it grows more elusive as the years pass. But if there is any truth to the tale, perhaps the slain innkeeper lingers within the Spence Inn as a forlorn ghost.

It's entirely possible that both the spiteful doctor and the murdered innkeeper find their souls trapped in the hotel, bound to the building by entirely different but equally tragic circumstances. Certainly there is enough unexplained activity to suggest the spectral register has more than one eternal guest written in it.

As the largest and perhaps most spiritually active building on the grounds of Muskoka Heritage Place, the Spence Inn plays a central role in the lantern-lit ghost walks Maria Da Silva and I lead at the museum every September. Unsurprisingly, it's the building in which most tour participants seem to feel hairs sticking up on the backs of their necks or ice-cold chills running down their spines. More than one person has refused to even climb the stairs to the darkened second floor.

Ian Russell, a founding member of a Hamilton-based paranormal investigation team called Ghost Hunt Paranormal, attended the ghost tour in 2016 with his partner, Trudy Shearing. He was in Muskoka house-sitting for a friend; the fact that it coincided with the timing of the ghost tour was a happy coincidence, one Ian and Trudy were all too happy to take advantage of.

"Whenever we go to a location, we always like to do a daytime walk-through to get a feel for the location, and the Muskoka pioneer village was no different. A few days prior to the tour, we spent the afternoon visiting the village and, during that time, experienced a ghostly encounter within the Spence Inn," Ian recalls. "As soon as we ascended the stairs to the second floor, we could feel a heavy energy occupying that upstairs level. Trudy was standing at the top of the stairs looking into the bedroom right across from the stairs. She turned and came face to face with a black shadow figure standing right in front of her at the top of the stairs. Was this the spirit of the doctor? We don't know."

Jump forward to the evening of the ghost walk itself: it was approaching 9:00 PM and the sun had long set, casting the village in darkness. Tour participants, Ian and Trudy among them, climbed onto the inn's porch and eagerly stepped through the door into the building, many subconsciously holding their breath in anticipation of being greeted by spectral energy. Some left disappointed, but not Ian and Trudy.

"Upstairs, Trudy felt as if someone was standing right behind her, following her, the entire time we were there. At one point she felt fingers running through her hair. I was focused on the doctor's office, holding an EMF detector through the doorway, and felt a cold breeze run over my hand," Ian recalls. The two paranormal investigators felt as if they had once again met the same ghost encountered during their earlier visit.

It's not just during the ghost tours, when the village is shrouded in the blackness of a Muskoka night and when people might be influenced by their own anticipation, that guests experience unusual things in the hotel. More often than not, they happen during the light of day when ghosts are far from people's minds. One story, for example, centres upon an American family exploring the pioneer village. Upon entering the Spence Inn the family separated, wandering singly and in pairs. One of the children, a 14-year-old girl, climbed the stairs and began exploring the second floor, snapping pictures of the guest rooms.

While photographing one room, she happened to look into an antique silver-rimmed mirror and was startled to see that it wasn't just her face reflecting back. Peering over her shoulder was the image of a jaundiced and bent corpse of a man, his skin speckled with age. Startled, she spun around to see who the angry old man standing behind her was. To her surprise, no one was there. She was alone, her body shaking with terror. Suddenly faint, she leaned against the wall with her eyes closed, chest heaving with ragged breaths. After long seconds trying to calm herself, she descended the stairs on unsteady legs and burst into tears as she told her parents about her terrifying encounter.

Staff members also report unusual, even chilling activity in the Spence Inn. One costumed staff member had an unusual experience that hinted strongly at spectral activity in the doctor's office. "I was on the ground floor of the inn when I heard a loud bang from above, somewhere on the second floor. It sounded like something had fallen, so I ran up the stairs and began searching the rooms for the source of the noise. I eventually found it: a big picture of a World War I soldier had fallen to the floor. There was no wind or vibration that could have knocked it loose; the hanger was still firmly set in the wall, and there was no one in the building who could have knocked it down as a prank. I couldn't figure it out; there was no explanation for it. I remember a dark feeling upstairs that day, and I didn't feel welcome there. Since then, others have experienced the same thing, and it's always the same picture."

Chilling experiences in the inn are nothing new and predate its relocation from Spence by decades. The museum archives have a letter indicating people had been complaining of spectral activity in and around the building during its time as a private residence. The most dramatic and frequent occurrence was the ghostly carriage that arrived in front of the inn during the middle of the night. There's evidence to suggest this phantom wagon continues to rattle along the Nipissing Road and always stops at the site where the Spence Inn stood.

One man sent me his experience via Twitter message. He was exploring the ghost towns along the Nipissing Road by car and had reached Spence late in the afternoon, just as the sun was dipping below the barren November trees. He heard a sound, quiet at first, then louder. The clip-clopping of hooves and the squeak of wagon wheels along the dirt road came nearer, but there was nothing to be seen. The sounds grew louder and louder, then suddenly seemed to stop right before the historic sign pinpointing the former location of the hotel. Now all was silent. The only sound to be heard was the wind blowing through the trees. Quietly, the man climbed back into his car and solemnly drove away, his day of exploration over. He, for one, is convinced that not every ghost associated with the Spence Inn made the move to Muskoka Heritage Place.

I've visited the Spence Inn after dark, alone, with only the light of a lantern to guide my way. I can testify that as you climb the stairs, an oppressive feeling threatens to overwhelm you. With each step taken, your heart races just a little faster and your nerves become balanced on a knife's edge. The floorboards creak and groan ominously. Shadows threaten to swallow you up. The dread becomes palpable. I got no farther than the top step before turning back, my courage failing me in an atmosphere that somehow felt wrong. That's the weight of history at work.

The Spence Inn was once a popular stop on long journeys. Perhaps it continues to be today, except that instead of weary stagecoach passengers, the guests filling the rooms are spirits trapped at the halfway point on the journey into the afterlife. In a tragic twist of irony, the hotel that once offered a welcome respite now serves as a prison for the souls of a long-dead innkeeper and physician who, for very different reasons, are incarcerated within this heritage structure.

Gabriel Blacksmith Shop: Crafting a Spectral Legend

The village blacksmith shop was once a common sight throughout Ontario. The air inside, thick with smoke and the scent of burning coal, is oppressively hot, sucking the breath from your lungs. The incessant ringing of hammer on anvil is almost maddening as metal is literally pounded into a new form. It's a hellish environment, one difficult enough to visit let alone spend a lifetime labouring within.

Blacksmiths were among the first skilled craftsmen to appear in any early Ontario community, and without their services, our society could never have developed. Yet several generations now have grown up not knowing the blacksmith shop and the importance of the smith to the pioneer economy. Frank Gabriel, for one, seems intent on reminding us. What's truly amazing is that Gabriel has been dead for half a century.

This story begins in Landkey, Devon, England, where Frank Gabriel was born on July 6, 1886, the seventh son of a wealthy butcher who owned five shops. Because he was the youngest son, Frank wasn't destined to inherit one of the butcher shops and instead had to find his own way in the world. At the age of 13 he was apprenticed to the village blacksmith and quickly became a master in the trade—so much so, in fact, that a mere two years later the 15-year-old was hired to assist in replacing the lead frames of some of the stained glass windows in Westminster Abbey in London.

In 1907, the 20-year-old blacksmith married Florence Jane Crook, a woman nine years his senior who was the product of an extremely well-to-do family distantly related to the British royal family. Indeed, with a twinkle in his eye, Frank would often boast later in life of being related to the queen. A year after being wed, John and Florence's first child, Olive May, was born. Another daughter soon followed. With two additional mouths to feed and Florence heavy with a third, and little in the way of prospects in England, Frank left for Canada in 1910. He did so with a heavy heart, however, because he had only enough money to purchase a ticket for himself; his wife and their children would have to join him at a later date.

In Canada, he saved every penny he could, dreaming about the day he would be reunited with his family. It took three years of hard work and deep loneliness for that dream to become a reality. With the Gabriel family together once more, Frank opened a blacksmith shop of his own in the community of Rockton. They remained there until 1926, when Frank moved his family again, this time to Novar in Parry Sound District, just north of Huntsville. Initially, Frank rented a blacksmith shop there from Jack McEwan, the proprietor of the village general store, but later he built a shop of his own from which to ply his trade.

It's easy to equate blacksmiths with horse shoeing and nothing more, but that provides an incomplete picture of blacksmiths' value to the community. In addition to forging horse shoes, they repaired farm equipment such as plows and furrows, crafted a variety of tools and farm implements and made houschold items such as pots and hinges. If the machinery at the local mill needed repair, the blacksmith was the one to call. In short, if the product was metal, a blacksmith was expected to be able to make and repair it. The blacksmith was almost certainly the most important artisan in any community, especially in Muskoka, where factory-made goods were expensive to come by and settlers farming this rugged landscape always short of money.

By the 1920s, blacksmiths were becoming increasingly rare and on the verge of obsolescence. Cars were replacing horses on the roadways of Ontario, farming was becoming increasingly mechanized, and factory-made goods were becoming more affordable and were quickly replacing those made by village craftsmen. Soon most blacksmiths had disappeared, the victims of changing times.

But Frank Gabriel endured, defying the passage of time. He continued to do good business in Novar. It helped that Muskoka, still something of a frontier region even at this late date, was slower in embracing change. Horses were still widely used on farms and in the logging industry, which meant an ongoing need for Gabriel's services. In addition, Gabriel made and repaired a lot of tools for loggers and made sleighs, wagons and buggies for residents.

By the late 1930s, the years of endless toil were taking a toll on Frank. The once strong man suffered from extreme arthritis in his hips and legs that caused him great pain. Years of supporting the weight of a horse's leg between his own while shoeing it had left his legs permanently bowed and crossed to the point of disfigurement. Frank was forced to walk with a pair of crutches—an indignity for the proud man. Still, he refused to give up the trade he loved.

Frank lost his beloved wife in 1956, and only a few years later he was forced by a degenerating body to finally give up his smithy. The dual blows were difficult to bear, but in his later years the artisan turned his attention to woodworking.

Shortly after his death on May 23, 1969, Frank's family donated his tools and squared-log home to Muskoka Heritage Place. There, the building was altered to appear as a blacksmith shop to educate modern visitors about the vital role these craftsmen played in the rural way of life as late as the mid-20th century. The blacksmith shop rapidly became the most popular building in the recreated community, the sound of hammer pounding on anvil echoing throughout the village and drawing in the public.

More than one visitor eager to watch a blacksmith at work has been stunned to find the shop empty, the hearth cold and no earthly source for the hammering. After spending a lifetime in his profession, Frank Gabriel continues to work away at his forge even decades after his death. One young museum employee I spoke to recalls hearing the spectral hammering on several occasions and being completely mystified by it. Having worked at the museum for several years, she was no stranger to the sounds of the village's resident blacksmith re-enactor at work, so there was no mistaking what she heard. The young woman recalls searching both inside and outside the smithy for the source of the sounds, finding nothing that could possibly explain them. They were paranormal.

One tourist, free of any knowledge of the rumoured spectral activity at the museum, saw the glow of a fire in the blacksmith shop one autumn day. Excited by the opportunity to see an authentic smith practicing a near-forgotten trade, he eagerly strode towards the smithy. When he drew nearer, the man was disappointed to see a crackling fire in forge, but no attending craftsman. He was somewhat surprised as well, thinking it a bit unsafe to leave an open fire unattended. Poking his head in the door, he looked around, wondering if perhaps the blacksmith was just out of view in one of the corners of the building. He looked to the left, toward the corner nearest the hearth and anvil. No one there. No one to the right. But in those seconds that he had turned his head, the flames mysteriously died and left in their wake no smoke, smell, ash or heat. It was if the fire had never existed. The visitor was further stunned to later discover that there was no blacksmith on site that day and the forge had therefore not been lit.

The spectral echo of the blacksmith at work in his forge is only one of the ways in which the paranormal world intrudes upon our own in this historic building. An amateur paranormal investigator entered the building one night during one of my annual ghost tours. She felt the distinct presence of someone lurking in the shadows that hovered just beyond the light cast by the lantern hanging from the rafters. The investigator said, "If you are here, let me know." She then felt a hand momentarily grip hers. She gasped in surprise. Later, when playing back her audio recorder, she heard a male voice reply to her query with a hollow-sounding "Yes." Just after that, the recording catches her gasping in surprise—right about when the ethereal hand grabbed hers. That same night, Elaine Matthews of Freelance Paranormal, an investigation team based in Muskoka, captured a number of unusual orbs in the blacksmith shop.

Some people claim to have heard the neighing of invisible horses in and around the blacksmith shop, an echo of the countless horses that Gabriel shod in his time. It should be pointed out that Dolly, the museum's resident donkey, has her corral nearby and it's possible that in some cases people are hearing her rather than something paranormal in nature. But do all the reported incidents have such an earthly origin?

If you believe in ghosts, you might expect to hear the disembodied sounds of hammers on metal, the pumping of the bellows or even the neighing of spectral horses waiting to be shod. But why would you hear conversations like those that might occur around the dinner table? Why the sound of children at play? These were the questions on the mind of a woman who distinctly heard these seemingly out-of-place sounds in the blacksmith shop.

But remember, although the museum doesn't advertise the fact anywhere, this building was never actually used as a blacksmith shop. Instead, it was Frank Gabriel's first home upon his move to Norval. It was only after being moved to the museum that it was transformed into a blacksmith shop, furnished of course with Gabriel's own tools. So sounds such as familial conversation and children playing aren't out of character for this building at all. Indeed, they are perfectly natural.

Some stories you hear can be chalked up to flights of fancy meant to inspire goosebumps. I was tempted to lump this one into the category of fiction as well until I interviewed Tony myself. A 70-odd-year-old who had seen a lot in his life, he came across as a no-nonsense kind of guy who was going to call them as he saw them. He visited the museum on a soggy day. A sort of mist was swirling that teetered on developing into rain. Tony entered the blacksmith shop and took comfort in the warmth of the fire while chatting amiably with the artisan at work.

A short while later, Tony said goodbye to the blacksmith and turned to leave—and almost bumped into another man standing just inside the yawning entrance. He was elderly, dressed in period clothes like those worn by the blacksmith re-enactor, with a wiry grey beard. He stood very stiff and erect, showing no sign of almost having been bumped into.

"Sorry," Tony gasped, startled by the man's sudden appearance. He hadn't sensed anyone behind him, nor had the blacksmith made any indication during their conversation that someone had entered the building.

Then Tony realized he could see the shape of the nearby hotel through the mysterious man. The view was distorted, like looking through the misty drizzle clouding the air, but there was no doubt the male figure was ethereal. The apparition took a silent step toward Tony, who stood there frozen in horror. And then a gust of wind blew into the smithy and carried away the ghost like wisps of smoke.

Tony started to breathe again, and finally his body began to respond to the commands his brain delivered. He turned toward the blacksmith, seeking solace in the comfort of another human being and looking for validation of the horror he had just experienced. He didn't find it. The blacksmith showed no sign of having seen anything untoward, which only made Tony feel colder and more alone.

My interview with Tony revealed he was completely unaware of the tradition of ghostly phenomena at Muskoka Heritage Place and moreover had absolutely no interest in the unexplained or in anything strange whatsoever. He had simply seen something that had frightened him—something for which he could find no explanation.

Andrew Dancy, a young man with an avid interest in the paranormal, participated in the September 2015 ghost tour at Muskoka Heritage Place. No moon or stars hung in the overcast sky. The wind whispered through the trees. The night air felt chill and damp. Midway through the tour, the group gathered in front of the blacksmith shop, huddling together in the light cast by the lanterns Maria Da Silva and I held aloft. The wind sighed. And then Dancy saw something that made him gasp.

"I saw a shadowy person step out from the back right corner of the building, then step back into the darkness a quick moment later. At first I wasn't completely sure of what I saw. It seemed unreal. I wondered if it might have been someone walking through the light. Funny thing is, when someone did walk by, they cast a shadow on the entire front of the building, blackening it all out. What I saw couldn't have been a member of the tour," Andrew recalls, noting how quickly it sank in that he had seen an apparition. "Funny to note: just after I thought I saw the shadow person, it was mentioned in the tour that a shadowy or darkish figure had been seen in that same corner of the building."

Though he isn't completely sure, Andrew believes he saw a glimpse of the spectral blacksmith cautiously peering out at the tour group, perhaps lamenting the intrusion of so many strange people into his home.

Frank Gabriel was an impressive man, so it's fitting that his blacksmith shop has been recreated among the dozen authentically restored buildings on display at Muskoka Heritage Place. He was so dedicated to his trade and so determined an individual that he continued to work at his forge even after crippling rheumatism began to wrack his body with pain. If anyone should have the strength of will to linger after death, it's Frank Gabriel. Perhaps he remains behind to remind us of his vanished trade, or more likely, to be near the fond memories this building held for him.

Ashworth Hall: Guarding Age-old Secrets

"Who are you?" Janet asked. She swallowed hard and stared wide-eyed at the shadowy figure standing motionless in the corner. He was tall and thin, with a tall hat upon his head. He studied Janet with cold, silvery eyes.

Afternoon sunlight shone through the open door. The light spread over the interior but seemed unable to penetrate into the corners—particularly the corner in which the mysterious shadow entity stood. Janet felt as if she were intruding upon a place where she didn't belong. She knew she had to leave, but she was frozen to the spot with fear.

Willing her leaden legs to obey her, she retreated from the building. Once back in the warmth of the sunlight, she felt safer. Nevertheless, she hastened down the earthen path. Janet put the building behind her, but she could not entirely escape the terror of the experience. She is just one of a handful of people who stumbled, quite unwillingly, upon the haunting legacy of Ashworth Hall at Muskoka Heritage Place.

Since time began, men have congregated in secret clubs and societies to fraternize, conduct business dealings and pool their resources to shape their communities to their liking. The number of these groups exploded during the 19th century. For every recognizable society, like the Freemasons or Shriners, there were dozens of obscure ones. The list was nearly endless, and they appeared in the largest of cities down to the smallest of villages.

Much of Muskoka in the 19th century was staunchly Protestant, inhabited almost solely by Englishmen. In 1800s Ontario, the expression of English ideals—Protestantism, Patriotism and Imperialism—was made concrete in the form of the Loyal Orange Lodge, a secretive and somewhat mysterious fraternity of men who conducted their affairs in private, away from the limelight and scrutiny of non-members. Most of the wealthiest, most prominent men in the area would be members, donning robes for their secret meetings at the lodges built by local chapters. Only rarely, during anniversaries of important events in Protestant history, would the members make public appearances together, often in parades or other shows of solidarity. But while the lodge was insular in nature, it looked outwards by quietly performing acts of benevolence and welfare. Families burned out of homes would receive assistance in rebuilding; farmers who suffered from poor crops were provided with food to sustain themselves through the harsh winter months; and the gravely sick were assured of medical attention regardless of their financial status.

Much of what was said within these lodges will forever remain a mystery. Most of the rituals and ceremony associated with the Victorian era of the Loyal Orange Lodge were lost to the pages of history as the society evolved and, with the improvement of roads linking disparate branches together, consolidated their practices. What secrets does Ashworth Hall, a former Orange Lodge, hold?

The simple, square-log hall was built in 1879 by Henry Demaine for Stanley Ashworth, a staunch Protestant who donated land and funds for a local Loyal Orange Lodge. By the 1890s, membership in the Ashworth Hall Orange Lodge had shrunk precipitously; age claimed some members, and others moved away owing to declining fortunes. The lodge closed in 1897.

The building remained vacant for the next two decades, but in 1920, Stanley Ashworth's son Edmund donated it to the local school board to replace the current rotting frame schoolhouse. The log hall was taken apart, hauled a few miles to the school grounds and then painstakingly reassembled. The former lodge served as a schoolhouse and community hall from 1921 to 1941, when it was closed and reverted back to the Ashworth estate. Years later, the building was moved one more time to its final home at Muskoka Heritage Place, where it was restored and furnished to recreate an authentic 19th-century Orange Lodge.

Even before its move to the museum, there were stories that the lodge was haunted by a dark man who stood silently in the building. He would intently watch those who entered, then a few long seconds later he would disappear into the shadows that linger in the corners of the building. These stories continued after the move to the museum. Even when the apparition isn't actually seen, some people report feeling a presence watching them as they tour the building.

Several encounters have occurred during the annual nighttime tours that I host with Maria Da Silva. Upon entering, the pale light cast by our lanterns does little to penetrate the dark corners of this log-hewn structure. Eyes strain to catch sight of the shadowy man to whom our storytelling has introduced guests just prior to stepping inside. To our knowledge, this ghost has never actually been seen during our tours, but he has made his presence known. One person captured the sound of a door closing and latching on her phone's audio recorder. The sound is distinct, but the lodge's door had remained open the entire time; there doesn't seem to be an earthly source for the sound. Two other people, a mother and her adult daughter, excitedly claimed to witness one of the Orangeman's purple robes that hang in the building flutter as if caught by a breeze. The night, however, while drizzly and chill, was perfectly still. What caused the robe to flutter? Finally, two separate teams of paranormal investigators noted that their electronic equipment inexplicably failed them upon entering the building, only to begin functioning without error after leaving.

No one knows who the ghost was in life. The most logical guesses are builder Henry Demaine or original owner Stanley Ashworth, both of whom were prominent members of the lodge and therefore would have had strong emotional attachments to it. Either seems a plausible identity for the lurking spirit.

In addition to the shadowy figure, there's another paranormal tradition linked to the building. Legend maintains that the organ would play a mournful tune of its own accord whenever a member of the lodge passed away. An Orangeman would breathe his last, and at that precise moment, anybody passing by would hear a haunting dirge escaping from the locked and shuttered lodge.

One eerie story from its time as a school seems to lend credence to what otherwise might be considered little more than folklore. One day in the 1920s, a local family was awoken in the early morning hours by the sound of an organ echoing across the landscape. The father pulled on pants and shirt, stepped into well-worn boots and grabbed a jacket as he went to investigate. Having grown up hearing tales of Ashworth Hall's haunted organ, the man was somewhat reluctant. He didn't consider himself a coward, but the idea of seeing the organ's keys moving under invisible fingers caused his hair to stand on end. Still, as a member of the community, he knew it was his responsibility to check on the school.

The man almost laughed at his own trepidation as he stepped into the early morning air. The landscape was covered in a fine mist, giving the light glowing in his home's windows a ghostly appearance. He shivered in the damp air and stomped towards the schoolhouse.

As he expected, the school was closed up tight, its front door locked and windows shuttered, with no light slipping out from under the door or between the shutters. And yet, though there was apparently no one inside, the organ played its mournful tune. It filled the man with fear.

He headed for home, eager for the warmth of his fireplace. He burst through the door but stopped suddenly when he saw his wife with tears running down her face. Her chin trembled. Her hands were clasped tightly in front of her.

"I'm so sorry," she said softly. "So sorry…"

"What's happened?"

His wife wrapped her arms around him. "I'm so sorry. It's your father. He died."

The man's head spun. He couldn't believe it. His father was a former member of the Orange Lodge, one of the last remaining Ashworth members. It was later revealed that the aging Orangeman had died in the early hours of the morning, shortly before the mysterious song was heard. The stories of the haunted organ were true after all.

As the one-time home of the Loyal Orange Lodge, Ashworth Hall guards its secrets well. These secrets are so deeply embedded into the logs of the hall that they have endured the building's changes in function, its several moves and the passage of more than a century of time. Will we ever determine the identity of the dark figure slinking among the shadows of Ashworth Hall? Is the legend of the haunted organ based on fact, or was it simply a tall tale told to children? Perhaps we'll never know the answer to these questions.

Hill House: Home for a Couple in Death as in Life

When we hear the term "haunted house," we instantly imagine something sinister and frightful: dried leaves crunching underfoot as we cautiously approach a dilapidated ruin of a home under the light of a full moon; an unnaturally cold wind whistling through trees that are leafless and bent; a sagging roof, diseased-looking vines strangling the walls, and mysterious forms looming ominously in windows; small animal bones hanging from the eaves like a sinister wind chime. That's the haunted house of popular culture. It's an image that looms large in our collective imagination, and it carries with it a powerful emotional impulse: fear, revulsion and sadness.

The Hill House is about as far from that picture as you're likely to find. A quaint, two-storey wooden structure tucked away at the back of the village at Muskoka Heritage Place, it's

Even in death, Reverend and Mrs. Hill continue to preside over their home.

warm and inviting, with neatly painted green trim, a welcoming entrance and impeccably maintained grounds. It's the epitome of Victorian-era charm, modest with attractive flourishes.

But appearances can be deceiving, for while it doesn't come near to the cliché imagery of a haunted house, the former home of Reverend Robert Norton Hill is very spiritually active. Those who knew Reverend Hill in life probably wouldn't be surprised to learn that he would defy the natural order by refusing to cross over to the other side. Indeed, staff unanimously agree that this charming home is the most haunted building at Muskoka Heritage Place.

Robert Norton Hill, born in 1825, was a Methodist preacher who spent the first half of his career ministering in the town of Schomberg. In 1867, he heard that free land was being offered in Muskoka as a means of encouraging settlement. Intrigued by the bountiful farms promised by the promotional literature and growing restless with his lot in Schomberg, the challenge of homesteading appealed to Hill. Here was a new frontier to conquer, and in this wild country there would surely be countless settlers eager for the comfort of faith. Hill resigned his ministry and, accompanied by his wife, Caroline, and their six children, headed north for Muskoka, where he hoped to find peace and contentment in working the land.

Hill had a vivid dream of his future homestead. He saw a spread of land jutting out into the crystalline water of a large lake, with an island directly in front of it. The dream was so real that Hill was certain it was a vision of the land fate intended for him. He set out in a canoe, paddling around a number of lakes in search of the landscape seen in his dream. Incredibly, along the unsettled shore of Peninsula Lake, just east of Huntsville, he discovered a location identical to the land he'd seen in his vision and knew it was meant for him. He quickly claimed the 700 acres of fine farmland and began the task of establishing a homestead.

The reverend played a significant role in extending civilization into the wilds of north Muskoka. The trail he blazed between Huntsville and his home, Hill's Trace, opened Peninsula Lake to settlement and became modern-day Highway 60. In 1878, he opened a post office he named Hillside; the village of Hillside inherited the name and considers Reverend Hill its founding father. Hill also worked as a government representative whose responsibilities included judging land disputes and the inspection of properties to confirm their compliance with the Free Grants and Homestead Act.

Although Reverend Hill had his hands full as a settler and government agent, he couldn't turn his back on God and his duty as a minister. Before long, he was tending to the spiritual needs for all of northern Muskoka, which required lengthy and exhausting journeys by foot, horseback and boat. Tired from his missionary work, Hill breathed his last in 1895, aged 70.

Almost a century later, Reverend Hill's home was moved to Muskoka Heritage Place to serve as an exhibit in the pioneer village. It seems Reverend Hill made the move as well, accompanied as always by his wife Caroline, from whom he was inseparable over half a century of marriage. A couple in death as they were in life, the Hills continue to reside in their charming home. Mrs. Hill seems confined to the second floor, leaving her husband to roam the dining room and drawing room on the ground floor by himself. They are generally quite content to share their home with hordes of tourists who visit the museum each summer, but not always.

"There was an entire year when nobody on staff would close the Hill House alone," recalls Teri Souter. "People heard footsteps upstairs when there was nobody else in the house, and even if they didn't hear anything they often felt that they were being watched."

The unnerving season Souter refers to is more than a decade in the past, and while the spectral activity has calmed somewhat in the interim, staff are still wary of the building. They say that the Hill House generally feels friendly and warm but admit there are times when a creepy essence clings to its walls like festering mould. It makes them uncomfortable and reluctant to be alone in the building after dark.

Many people walking through the village have sensed the presence of a woman watching them from an upstairs window, seen an ethereal hand pulling back a bedroom curtain or caught a momentary glimpse of an elderly lady tentatively peeking through the glass at an unfamiliar world. Often there will be an indentation in the quilt of the master bedroom, as if someone had been—or perhaps is still—sitting there. Staff members swear the indentation isn't there in the morning and that it forms by itself during the day, always in the same spot. Soft footsteps and even a muffled woman's voice have been heard, but there's never anyone there. The door to Mrs. Hill's bedroom even swung shut once on its own, not just swinging on its hinges but actually completely closing. There was no wind, no breeze, no natural phenomenon that could have been responsible.

The most memorable incident involving the spirit of Mrs. Hill occurred in autumn 2001 during a Halloween event geared towards youngsters. The village was alive with the sound of children's laughter as dozens of little ones raced from building to building, thrilled by the novel setting and festive activities. Perhaps all the noise and youthful energy annoyed old Mrs. Hill because she acted out in an uncharacteristic fashion.

A group of children entered the Hill House, followed closely by their adult guardians. While most of the kids remained downstairs, several others raced upstairs with two women close on their heels to ensure they didn't get into any mischief. The women kept a watchful eye on the exploring kids but took the time to peer into the bedrooms and appreciate the history they represent.

While peeking into the master bedroom, an antique hairbrush sitting atop a dresser caught the eye of the women. It was beautiful and ornate, clearly a prized heirloom, but what got their attention was the way it rattled and shook even though everything else on the dresser remained perfectly still. Suddenly, to their astonishment, the hairbrush flew off the dresser and past their faces, landing a couple of metres away. Now frightened, they hurriedly gathered up the children and raced downstairs, where they shared their experience with Sara White, the museum's collections manager who happened to be working as a costumed interpreter that night. Sara recalls that the women were clearly scared, with pale faces, wide eyes, shaking hands and quivering voices.

Details of the evening's excitement eventually reached Teri Souter, who was taken aback by the tale. She remembered being told by a Hill descendant that Caroline Hill had had long, beautiful hair, of which she was extremely proud and which, even in old age, she would spend countless hours brushing. The fact that it had been her brush that had been flung across the room couldn't have been a coincidence. Had Mrs. Hill been upset at having her evening disturbed by noisy children? It seems likely.

An eerily similar event happened a few years later when a woman named Bobbi visited the museum with her teenaged daughter. While taking photos of the master bedroom in the Hill House, Bobbi watched through the camera's viewfinder as the hairbrush slowly levitated several inches into the air. She gasped. A split second later, the brush dropped back to the dresser. Overwhelmed by a rising tide of fear, Bobbi ran from the room, almost knocking her daughter down in her haste to escape.

Julie participated in one of the yearly the lantern-lit ghost tours Maria Da Silva and I lead through the museum. She is passionately interested in the paranormal and had been looking forward to the event for weeks. She got her money's worth—and more!

When we entered the Hill House, I placed a lantern at the top of the narrow staircase on the second floor to ensure people had something to see by as they explored. I then went to the bottom of the stairs to wait for the tour to filter through the building.

Perhaps 10 minutes later, Julie was alone upstairs. She wanted it that way so she could experience the building free of the crowd and the noise that came with it, reasoning this was the only way she could possibly experience anything paranormal.

The floorboards groaned under Julie's shoes as she made her way down the dimly lit hall. The air was damp and chill. She peered into rooms, but the light shed by the lantern sitting at the top of the stairs didn't penetrate far, so she couldn't see much.

But what was that noise? Was someone else upstairs with her? It sounded like quiet footsteps, as if someone was padding carefully down the hall. Yet she saw no one. Julie listened carefully. She heard the sound again. Was someone trying sneak up on her in an attempt to startle her?

"Is someone there?" she called out.

No reply.

A chill tingled the back of her neck. It was time to leave and rejoin the tour group below. She began to hurry down the hall, but stopped when she heard a cough. It sounded like it came from directly behind her. She spun around. Her eyes strained to penetrate the shadows, but there was no one in sight. She slowed her breathing and strained her ears to listen.

Silence.

Now she'd had enough. Her courage failing her, she raced down the stairs and exited the building, passing me on the way out. She was indeed the last member of the tour group on the second floor. There was no one—at least no one of this world—upstairs who could have made the noises she described.

Incredibly, Reverend Hill's spirit is widely believed to be more strongly imbued than his wife's within the home. This perhaps makes sense, in light of his strength of character in life. Though not malicious, he seems to like reminding people that he's the man of the house and as such deserves respect. When respect isn't forthcoming, or when Reverend Hill simply wants his privacy, he acts out in an attempt to drive people off.

One summer day, a staff member heard the home's front door creak open and then close shut. Heavy footsteps made their way towards the drawing room. The footfalls were slow and loud, as if made by a large man who was either old or tired. When the footsteps reached the drawing room, they stopped. The staff member, in the kitchen at the time, poked her head into the drawing room, prepared to greet a guest. She was surprised to find no one in sight. Thinking perhaps the visitor had silently exited the building, she peered out onto the grounds. Not a soul was in view. Confused, she went back inside and searched the entire building, but the Hill House was empty. She had no explanation for what she heard; the footsteps were loud and distinct and couldn't have been confused for anything else.

There's a big wooden chair in the kitchen that seems to be a favourite of Reverend Hill's. People often sense a powerful otherworldly presence sitting in it, and some who touch the chair have been known to feel a shiver run up their spine. Once, on a hot, muggy summer's day without a hint of breeze, stunned visitors watched as the chair began rocking back and forth all on its own. It creaked forward then back again, as if propelled by an unseen body, at least four or five times.

One gentleman visiting the museum once made the mistake of sitting in the chair. He was hot and tired from walking and wanted to take a load off his aching feet, but as soon as he settled in the chair, he felt uncomfortable and intuitively knew that someone strongly objected to him sitting there. He jumped to his feet and quickly left the building, wanting to put distance between himself and the riled spirit. Was the reverend angered by an uninvited guest making himself so casually at home?

Reverend Hill even posed for a photo once. This incident took place years ago, when several dozen members of the extended Hill family converged on Muskoka Heritage Place for a family reunion. For many of them, it was their first time seeing the home in which their common ancestors had lived. Later that day, before people began to filter away, everyone posed for a family portrait outside the Hill House. The photo was taken, people embraced and wished one another well, and the reunion ended.

But the mystery was just beginning. When the photo was developed some weeks later, a man no one could identify was in the picture, posing along with the rest of the assembled family members. He had a thick, wiry beard, dark eyes, a somewhat stern countenance and was wearing a stark, black suit. No one could remember this man being there. Finally, after all logical explanations had been discarded, it slowly began to be accepted that the individual was actually an apparition. Someone had the idea to look through old family photos, and sure enough they found the mystery guest among them: the long-dead Reverend Robert Norton Hill himself.

Ghostly experiences are so commonplace in the Hill House that it has become something of a tradition to greet the Hills in the morning and say good night to them at the end of the day. Even those who claim not to believe in the paranormal take time for this courtesy, just in case. Better to be safe than risk offending a potentially wrathful spirit, after all.

Every community, it seems, has a haunted house to call its own. The pioneer village at Muskoka Heritage Place is no different. Hill House may not look anything like a traditional haunted house, but make no mistake: this home has spectral residents who aren't shy. You're welcome to see for yourself. Just make sure to greet the homeowners upon entering.

See For Yourself

Each of the nearly two dozen buildings at Muskoka Heritage Place has a spirit all its own, the product of the successes and failures, happiness and heartache of the men and women who lived and worked within them. In that light, it shouldn't be surprising that spectral energy lurks in the cracks between well-worn floorboards, seeping out on occasion to startle staff and guests alike.

Muskoka Heritage Place is the greatest repository of history in Ontario's Cottage Country District, a worthy destination for anyone. But it's a repository of ghost stories as well, some so frightful that never a word was spoken—until now.

∼

Enlistments that Last an Eternity: The Carleton Martello Tower

~

High on a hill above Saint John, New Brunswick, looms the squat shape of a stone tower built by the British in the early 1800s. Intended to protect the city during the War of 1812, it played a significant role during the mid-19th-century Fenian Crisis and in both World Wars of the 20th century. The structure also bears the distinction of being the oldest building in the city. To say that history endures within the Carleton Martello Tower is a gross understatement; even after 200 years, it continues to stand sentinel over Saint John.

Also standing sentinel over the city are a number of spectral soldiers who remain on duty long after their terms of enlistment should have ended. These apparitions, who hail from a number of eras and wear starkly different uniforms, have one thing in common: a part of their soul has cemented itself to the mortar of the tower itself, binding them to the site perhaps forever.

Talk with any of the staff members. They are happy to while away a summer's afternoon sharing the history of the tower. They may even tell you all about the ghosts. What follows are the stories you'd hear.

During the War of 1812, when the United States declared war against Great Britain and launched a number of invasions in Canada, it was deemed necessary to protect Saint John. Not only was the city New Brunswick's largest and most important port, but it also offered an overland route to Canada's interior that was especially vital when the St. Lawrence froze during winter. Royal Engineers recognized Carleton Heights, a rocky cliff overlooking the western land approaches to the city, as the most strategic location to site the planned fortification—this hilltop position was the perfect vantage point from which to defend Saint John against attack.

In 1813, Royal Engineers began construction of a unique style of fortification known as a Martello tower. Martello towers, hundreds of which were built all over the British Empire, had certain features in common. All were circular in shape with a flat roof on which artillery could be mounted to fire down upon advancing troops or naval vessels. The towers were accessible through a doorway in the second storey, which served as barracks for the troops manning the tower. The ground floor had storage space and a gunpowder magazine. The key feature was a round brick pillar that supported both the roof and the arched brick ceiling which, along with the thick walls, was designed to absorb artillery fire.

The Carleton Martello Tower measures 9 metres high and 15 metres in diameter. It was the final link in a chain of three fortresses (the others being Fort Howe, protecting the river, and Fort Dufferin, guarding the harbour entrance near Partridge Island) protecting the city from attack. The British had planned to install artillery guns on the tower, but nothing came of these plans; the fort was only completed in spring 1815, weeks after the War of 1812 had ended.

Nonetheless, the Carleton Martello Tower saw extensive use over the next century and a half. In 1866, there was a very real fear that Saint John would be attacked by the Fenian Brotherhood, a radical Irish-American group that hoped to capture British North America as ransom for Irish independence. This threat resulted in a small detachment of British soldiers from the 15th Regiment of Foot being stationed at the tower until 1867. Also, the tower was armed with artillery for the first time since it had been built, with two large smooth-bore guns manned by the New Brunswick Regiment of Garrison Artillery positioned atop its flat roof.

The tower was next used during World War I, but not in a defensive role. Instead, it incarcerated approximately 50 men who attempted to desert from the 69th Battalion rather than face the grim reality of life in the trenches on the Western Front. These desperate men were confined in cold, stark conditions from November 1915 until April 1916, when the unit—the would-be deserters included—finally shipped overseas.

With the outbreak of World War II, the security of Saint John was once again a top concern. Although not a major naval base, the city did have a large dry dock and was the end point for Europe-bound supplies travelling across the country by rail. In late 1939, the 8th Anti-Aircraft Battery placed machine guns on the upper level of the tower against a feared air attack from German bombers, and the tower also served as a fire command post for coastal artillery batteries ringing the harbour. In August 1941, a two-storey concrete structure was built on the roof to accommodate communication and tracking equipment. Manning the tower were soldiers of the 3rd New Brunswick Coast Brigade. After the Battle of Normandy ended in August 1944, any Nazi threat to Saint John was deemed to have passed, and military operations at the tower ceased—this time for good.

During the entirety of its service as a military bastion, not a single soldier died at the Carleton Martello Tower. There are literally hundreds of documents and newspaper articles chronicling the history of the fort and the service of those stationed within. Nowhere is there a mention of any foul deed that may have given cause to keep souls from their graves. And yet people claim to have accidentally confronted wandering spirits and witnessed eerie poltergeists there.

Edward hails from Ontario but has deep maritime roots. Every few years, he feels the pull of the jagged seacoast and returns to reconnect with his roots. During one such visit, he and his wife visited Saint John and toured the Carleton Martello Tower.

The couple was approaching the tower's stout stone walls when they came upon a re-enactor standing in their path. He wore a blue uniform with a wide-brimmed hat. A distinctive red scarf hung loosely around his neck, and he had a rifle slung over his shoulder. The soldier smiled, stepped aside to let Edward and his wife pass and tipped his hat in greeting. Edward recalls saying hello as they passed.

A short while later, while inside the tower exploring the barracks floor, another costumed re-enactor approached them and offered to tell them a bit about the life of soldiers garrisoned there in the 19th century. During the conversation, Edward asked whether the other staff member outside would be demonstrating the firing of his musket sometime that afternoon. He'll never forget the quizzical look on the other man's face. He was the only staff member on duty at the time. It seems the other soldier was from another time. Who was he while on this earth? What was his name and how did he die? We will likely never know.

It's said that poltergeist activity occasionally plagues the barracks. Soft whispers might be blamed on the maritime breeze rolling in off the Bay of Fundy, but how does one explain the wooden canteen that fell, or more accurately was thrown, off its peg to land several feet away? Or the tin mug that rattled on the wooden table? Such things are harder to rationalize away.

Another tourist who I will call Laura had a brief but nonetheless spine-tingling experience in the tower. Although she has a long history of sensing spiritual energy, she was wholly unprepared for what she felt in the tower. Upon entering, Laura was rocked back on her heels and almost overwhelmed by a malignant darkness. The interior of the tower is well lit, but she sensed gloom and shadow. She "saw" a soldier pacing in an endless circle, damned to an eternity of imprisonment and emotional torture for some misdeed. The raw energy Laura sensed was too much for her; she left, tears streaming down her cheeks and hands trembling with fear.

Laura has no further details to offer. The power of the emotions she sensed blocked her ability to read anything else from the spirit, so we cannot rely on her impressions to guide us in unearthing more about the tortured soul. However, based upon her description it seems fair to say that the soldier may be one of the deserters from the 69th Battalion back in 1915. Maybe the spirit is restless because he died on foreign soil in a war he had no desire to participate in. Or perhaps the tower has held onto the powerful emotions of the deserters—fear, anxiety, desperation, even shame—for the past century and exhales them like foul breath on occasion. Either of these tragic explanations seems equally possible.

As the legend continues to unfold and sightings of the spirits at the Carleton Martello Tower continue, we can only hope to discover more about them and their lives and, maybe more importantly, what happened in death that causes their coffins to spit out their souls.

See For Yourself

One of only nine remaining Martello-style towers in Canada, the Carleton Martello Tower is richly deserving of its designation as a National Historic Site. It's also deserving of an afternoon of your time.

Begin your exploration by learning about the tower's history through award-winning, interactive exhibits and a documentary film in the visitor centre, then guide yourself through the tower and grounds, including barracks replicating the living conditions of a 19th-century British soldier and the powder magazine where ammunition was stored.

During the summer months, re-enactments both entertain visitors and help them to better envision a soldier's life. Costumed interpreters demonstrate military drills, mock attacks and weapons handling, and then guests may try on heavy woollen uniforms and join in the simulated action.

Military history isn't the only reason people visit Carleton Martello Tower. Peaceful opportunities factor in as well. Don't miss the panoramic view from the lookout, where you can snap photos of vessels bobbing on the water in Saint John Harbour, dramatic vistas out to the Bay of Fundy and, on a clear day, the distant silhouette of Nova Scotia. It's a great place to pack a picnic and revel in the fresh maritime breeze.

Special events are held throughout the season. Most notable for readers of this volume are their ghost walks that pull back history's curtain to reveal some of the creepy and tragic tales associated with this heritage site.

The Art Gallery of Sudbury: A Proud and Paranormal Legacy

~

Wi illiam Bell led an extraordinary life, filled with enterprise and philanthropy. Although he was himself a product of the lumber industry, he helped Sudbury transition from a rough-around-the-edges logging community to a modern town with all the niceties of civilization. While Bell's legacy in Sudbury is impressive and his achievements many, the most concrete reminder of his life is his former home, the Bell Mansion, now home to the Art Gallery of Sudbury. Based on the man's prominence, is it little surprise that William Bell's home is among the most haunted in Sudbury?

Born in Pembroke in 1858, William Bell left home as a teenager to work in logging camps, where he felled trees over winter and drove logs down swollen rivers in spring. Working his way up from lumberjack to camp foreman and showing considerable business acumen, he later moved into management positions. In 1886 he married 23-year-old Katherine Skead, the well-educated and headstrong daughter of senator and businessman James Skead.

William Bell spent most of his first four decades in and around Pembroke, but in 1896, he and his wife followed the logging industry west to Sudbury to take up the position of manager of the Sable and Spanish River Boom and Slide Company. Five years later, he was vice president and general manager of the Spanish River Lumber Company, the largest of almost

40 logging operations along the north shore of Lake Huron. By 1924, after purchasing a controlling interest in the company, he had established logging operations along Lake Wanapitei. An adoring husband, William named the community that housed his lakeside operations Skead in honour of his wife. Bell also entered into partnership with William Benjamin Arnold to form Arnold and Bell, another logging operation on the north shore of Lake Huron.

Seeking a route to fortune beyond the lumber industry—which, as an astute businessman, Bell knew was profitable only so long as the harvestable lumber lasted—Bell turned to merchandising. He partnered in the Cochrane-Dunlop Hardware Company and founded National Grocers Ltd., which imported staple supplies to what was still a remote community. Such business endeavours resulted in a prosperous life.

William built an opulent mansion in Sudbury to serve as a reflection of his wealth and standing. No expense was spared to create a home that was the envy of Sudbury, a home that he and the entire community could be proud of.

But riches weren't enough for the large, powerfully built, always impeccably dressed man. He wanted to be respected in the community, a leader in society as well as in industry. To that end he gave his time and money to support St. Andrew's United Church, where he served as secretary and treasurer; was prominent in the Masonic Lodge; helped bring the Rotary Club to Sudbury; was instrumental in the formation of Idylwylde Golf Club (golf being a game he passionately loved, as much because it signalled he was a "gentleman" as for the game itself) and was an active member of the Sudbury Hockey Club; financed Sudbury's first theatre, the Grand Theatre, with 14 other men; and, as a member of Sudbury's Park Department, advocated for the creation of local parks, going so far as to donate the land for Memorial Park.

All of Sudbury mourned when William Bell passed away at the age of 87 on January 12, 1945, due to complications from a leg injury. Thousands attended the funeral, recognizing they had lost a loyal, honourable citizen. He left one last gift to Sudbury in the form of a $125,000 gift to the Salvation Army for the construction of a men's centre on Larch Street.

In light of William's standing in and commitment to the community, when one hears that his mansion is haunted by a restless spirit, you'd be tempted to assume it is he who wanders the halls under the cover of darkness, refusing to accept that he is no longer the man of the house. Some say he does occasionally make himself known, but it's his beloved wife Katherine, a woman in many ways as strong-willed as he, who refuses to loosen her grip on the Bell Mansion.

Like her husband, Katherine was very active in Sudbury. She was a leading figure in St. Andrew's United Church, founded the Victorian Order of Nurses in Sudbury and served as its president, was at the centre of a number of women's social groups and was responsible for starting the Sudbury Horticultural Society. She volunteered her time to the Children's Aid Society and the Sudbury Public Library. Katherine loved animals, and she campaigned tirelessly to ensure horses working in her husband's lumber camps were treated humanely. Indeed, she rarely rode in her husband's opulent car, preferring instead her horse-drawn buggy even after such a sight was extremely rare in Sudbury.

It's been written that while Katherine was a benefactor of a number of causes, she couldn't bring herself to give as generously when it came to initiatives aimed at children because she despised little ones. This assertion is simply not true. Her inability to have children of her own only encouraged Katherine to volunteer her time and money to the Children's Aid Society.

Widowed at the age of 82, Katherine remained in the Bell Mansion until her death on January 9, 1954, aged 91. When she passed, she willed the mansion to Memorial Hospital. It served briefly as a nurse's residence until it was gutted by a fire on December 3, 1955. When at last the fire had died out and the smoked cleared, the gawking crowds that had flocked to the scene were stunned by the level of destruction. The once opulent home, a Sudbury landmark, had been reduced to a pile of sizzling embers and charred beams within the stout stone walls. There was hardly a dry eye in the crowd.

In the aftermath of the inferno, the Nickel Lodge Masons purchased the building from Memorial Hospital. They hoped to rebuild, but in the end nothing came of their ambitions. Instead, the Bell Mansion sat idle, the doors and windows boarded up, the inside a blackened and charred ruin.

Thankfully, that wasn't the end of the story. In 1966, after sitting empty and neglected for over a decade, the property was purchased by the Centennial Committee of the Chamber of Commerce. Renovations began shortly thereafter, returning the mansion to a semblance of its former grandeur. In 1968, it was officially transferred to Laurentian University, which now leases the space to the art gallery. In such a way, the building has been returned to a position of prominence in the community—fitting for the one-time home of a couple who played such an important role in early Sudbury.

Although the mansion has long been out of Bell hands, apparently Katherine never really left. She was particular about her house and might be watching over it and its occupants. Most staff members agree that if you spend enough time in the gallery, any previously held skepticism about the existence of ghosts will be extinguished.

One employee served in the mansion for over four years, and during that time she experienced enough paranormal encounters to convince even the most rational of minds. More than once she was left staring wide-eyed at something unexplainable, felt her spine shiver at the haunting sound of something otherworldly or was left casting nervous glances over her shoulder when she sensed eyes boring into her. She explains, "I didn't believe in ghosts when I began working at the gallery. I soon changed my mind. Things happened frequently, maybe as often as once or twice a month. The first few times something happened I'd look for an explanation and be startled when no explanation could be found. I started to question my beliefs, even my sanity. Eventually I was forced to accept that there is life after death, but I never really got used to it, and the fear never really went away."

At times, security guards have heard phantom footsteps moving through the gallery in the wee hours of the night. At such a late hour, they know there are no staff in the building who could be walking around. The guards thoroughly search the building for any breach in security but never find anything out of order. Sometimes guards hear violent sounds of crashing from the second floor, as if a piece of artwork has fallen off the wall, but they never find anything out of place.

At other times, the ghostly activity is more obvious to the living. Items have inexplicably disappeared, much to the frustration of staff, only to turn up again a few days later in spots where they couldn't have been overlooked. Then there was the day a staff member came into the gallery in the pre-dawn hours to get a head start on an important task: "I heard noises downstairs. It sounded like indistinct voices talking together, the sounds of multiple people walking, the front door opening and closing and horses neighing outside. I ran downstairs, and the noises stopped." Were Katherine Bell and friends heading out for a ride in her carriage?

Still don't believe in ghosts? One staff member who worked at the gallery in the early 1990s didn't…at least until she decided to put the ghost to the test one day. She had heard so much about wandering spirits and spooky sounds, but after months of employment had never experienced anything even remotely strange. Shortly after the museum had closed for the day, when the shadows were gathering outside and the stillness of night was settling, the woman knocked twice on an interior wall. "If you're here, can you do *that*, Mrs. Bell?" She was kind of mocking her co-workers' naivety for believing in ghosts and smiled at her own cleverness.

Then the wall knocked back. *Rap, rap*—two knocks in a row, just as she had done moments before. The smile drained from her face, along with all colour. Chastened and frightened, the woman hurriedly left the building. She never again doubted the presence of a ghost within the Bell Mansion.

One local woman who took a job as a security guard for the gallery shared a hair-raising evening she endured while on duty. Shortly after the gallery closed for the evening, the guard began her rounds to ensure no one remained in the building and that everything was secure. The path she took was the same every night. She would begin in the basement and then climb two flights of stairs past the ground floor to the second storey, which held galleries two and three. The routine was just that— routine. But this night was anything but routine.

Finding nothing amiss in the basement, the security guard made her way upstairs. She had just turned off the lights in Gallery 3 and was walking back through Gallery 2 to return to the stairs when she stopped suddenly in mid-step, frozen. Something was off.

The skin on the back of her neck tingled. She could sense someone's presence and feel eyes watching her from behind. The sensation was unnerving and frightening. She turned her head, looking back to the gallery she had just left. The guard's breath caught in her throat as she watched the apparition of a woman in Edwardian dress striding purpose-fully, perfectly at home, across the floor through the doorway leading to Gallery 3. The ghost looked like a flesh-and-blood person, not misty or ethereal, but the security guard instantly recognized her. It was Katherine Bell. Terrified, the guard raced down the stairs two at a time and bolted through the front door, stopping only long enough to lock the gallery before retreating to the safety of her home.

Not all encounters with Mrs. Bell end with someone fleeing in terror. Indeed, some are almost warm and soothing. Some people have heard a pleasant woman's voice singing throughout the mansion, as if the woman of the house is rehearsing for an otherworldly concert. While her lyrical voice has been heard floating through halls all over the gallery, the conservatory seems to the nexus for these spectral recitals. Maybe with good reason: the conservatory, with its tiled floors and large windows, is the only room that survived the 1955 fire. Katherine Bell may well have hosted parties and recitals in this very room.

Sometimes Mrs. Bell will even respond when someone else sings, forming a duet across two planes—the living and the dead. Perhaps she misses the church concerts and social evenings she organized while alive and longs to be accompanied by another singer. Take this encounter for example: "It had been a relatively quiet day at work, but as early evening set in, the atmosphere changed. It seemed charged somehow. I had finished my paperwork for the day's shift and wandered into the gallery from the guard station, admiring the exhibit that was on display," this female security guard explains. "Sometimes, when there weren't any visitors at all in the gallery, I would stand in the middle of Gallery 1 and just sing. I loved the acoustics. I know, it doesn't sound professional, but when you're faced with a bit of fear, an empty gallery and rumours of ghosts, well, singing loudly seems to settle my nerves."

On this particular night while singing to soothe her nerves, the woman heard a humming sound. She stopped singing and stood motionless, just listening. "It wasn't a steady hum, but it had the lyrical sounds and structure of a song. Soon, the humming seemed to morph into something stronger, stringing itself through Gallery 1 and moving up the stairs. It was a woman's voice. It was soft and distant, but it was there." She concluded that Mrs. Bell was singing in response to her own singing. Far from being frightened, the guard was happy for the duet.

William may also make his presence known on occasion. According to local lore, the former owner checks on the building at night. His footsteps and taps are heard in the rooms. A shadowy man wearing a dark suit and top hat was once seen standing in a corner, watching art lovers browsing the gallery for a while before disappearing in the blink of a disbelieving eye.

Inexplicably, in the years immediately after the house was rebuilt, people swore they heard the joyful sound of children laughing and playing inside. Why? William and Katherine Bell were fated never to have children of their own, so their home never saw young ones at play. No one, apparently, has heard these ghostly children for decades, but nagging questions remain. Have these spectral kids moved on, or are they simply behaving themselves? Who were they in life, and how were they connected to the Bell Mansion?

Memories and emotions remain behind to mark our passing. This is certainly the case at the Art Gallery of Sudbury. While it's been devoted to the arts for half a century, the building hasn't completely shaken its ties to the couple who made it for a time the heart of business and society in Sudbury. The bond between William and Katherine Bell and their home cannot be broken, even after the curtain of death descended upon the couple. Katherine's presence is particularly strong. She lingers for love...love of home, love of community and the love between husband and wife that these brick walls represent.

See For Yourself

The Art Gallery of Sudbury is a community treasure. As the former home of a local lumber baron, it has unique historic and architectural appeal. Step through the front doors of the heritage building and enter an oasis of local art, both historical and contemporary, and including works from First Nations people of northern Ontario. Exhibits change frequently, ensuring the gallery remains fresh and maintains its mandate as a vibrant place for ongoing engagement with the visual arts.

The Art Gallery of Sudbury is more than just a place to view artwork; it's also a place to experience artwork, through frequent art classes, lecture series and interactive events designed to encourage a passion for the arts.

Fort Fear: Ghosts of Fort Battleford

~

The tour guide warmly greeted the group he was to lead through Fort Battleford. The group was large, consisting of two adult sisters, their husbands and their children, who ranged in age from 12 years down to two cute-as-a-button three-year-old girls. The guide felt an immediate connection to the two little ones, and as the tour progressed he pulled out a hand puppet, Harry the Horse, to entertain them. Harry was such as success that, despite their young age, the little girls remained engaged even after the tour had explored two of the on-site historic buildings. Everyone was having a great time.

And then it happened. As one of the girls crossed the threshold into the next building, she started to scream. Her eyes were as large as saucers and she wailed in pain, as though someone was hurting her. She threw herself to the ground and writhed on the wooden floorboards. "Make him go away," she wailed, tears rolling down her chubby cheeks. "I scared, Mommy!"

The terrified youngster pushed at the air above her as if something horrific loomed over her, closing in with malicious intent. She screamed and struggled and cried in obvious distress. Her dad raced to her side, picked her up and cradled her to his chest. The concerned guide suggested he take his daughter outside to get some air.

As soon as the girl was away from the building, she immediately calmed. But if her father tried to bring her back in to rejoin the group, she would begin to panic anew. Her father couldn't make sense of what troubled his child, but the guide knew. He explained to the family that there had been a violent death in that building in the distant past, that the building was haunted and that staff and other visitors had had similar reactions to the spiritual energy therein.

Although the family was troubled by the girl's reaction, they were comforted in knowing she was far from the only one to have a terrifying experience at Saskatchewan's Fort Battleford, a historic site that's almost certainly the most haunted location in the province. No one should be surprised the dead rest uneasily here; it is the site of the largest mass hanging in Canadian history, a dubious distinction that has left a dark stain on the land and its buildings.

Fort Battleford was instrumental in some of the most pivotal events in the history of western Canada. The ghosts that linger at the fort, just out of sight but never far away, are tied to these often tragic events. To understand the pain and torment that fuel the hauntings, one must understand the fort's history.

By the 1870s, the North-West Territories (a vast swath of land formerly owned and administered by the Hudson's Bay Company consisting of Saskatchewan, Alberta, most of modern-day Manitoba and the northern territories) were opening up for European settlement. Hundreds of land-hungry migrants arrived each year, pulling handcarts holding their worldly possessions. Farmsteads began to dot the prairie homeland of the nomadic Native tribes; plowed fields interrupted ancestral hunting grounds, and grazing cattle competed for forage with the bison that formed the bulk of the Native diet. In retrospect, some sort of clash of cultures was inevitable.

One of the towns that emerged during this early period of settlement was Battleford, in what is now west-central Saskatchewan. When it was named the capital of the North-West Territories in 1876, the North-West Mounted Police (NWMP) established a fort nearby to provide security and ensure rule of law. In addition to guarding the largest and wealthiest town in the Canadian West, it protected the North Saskatchewan and Battle rivers, which were vital transportation routes in this vast region. And, at the time, the Canadian Pacific Railway was supposed to pass through Battleford on its way to the west coast (in the end, the route was diverted farther south, and the capital was moved to Regina as a result).

Fort Battleford, the sixth NWMP fort to be built in the North-West Territories, occupied a strategic position atop a high plateau. It was easily defensible and offered clear lines of sight of the surrounding area for ample warning against possible attacks. A sturdy wooden palisade enclosed 10 buildings, including officers' quarters, a barracks, a storehouse, a workshop and stables, in an area measuring 145 metres by 155 metres.

The government's hope was that the presence of the NWMP would act as a moderating influence on the First Nations in the area and help them to transition from their nomadic lifestyle to a more sedentary one modelled on European societies. They also hoped that the force would assist settlers in their homesteading efforts, and that a police presence in the area would encourage settlers to respect the law so as to prevent the lawlessness and violence that characterized the American West. And in general, settlement proved largely peaceful. There were exceptions, however, and Fort Battleford played a pivotal role in one of them: the 1885 Northwest Rebellion.

The late 19th century was a difficult time for the First Nations and Metis on the prairies. Wild game was scarce, and the bison upon which they traditionally sustained themselves were almost extinct. The First Nations had negotiated treaties with the Crown, but the food, equipment and training that had been promised to assist them in taking up agriculture and abandoning their traditional lifestyle was not always forthcoming or of good quality. Many bands existed on bare subsistence. Petitions for government assistance fell on deaf ears, and tension and frustration inevitably grew. Finally, after a particularly cold and hungry winter, the tensions that had been simmering for so long reached a boil: in March 1885, the Metis and some Native bands rose up in rebellion against the government.

"What's important to remember is that we refer to these events as the Northwest Rebellion, and certainly the government considered the events of 1885 as a single uprising, but in fact they were related by separate episodes. The Metis of Saskatchewan rose up under the leadership of Louis Riel, while a small number of First Nations warriors went against their chiefs and rose in rebellion," explains Tami Conley-Blais, interpretation officer at Fort Battleford National Historic Site.

Fighting began on March 26 when 100 NWMP officers attempted to disperse and disarm a force of about 250 Metis just outside the community of Duck Lake, not far to the east of

Battleford. A fierce firefight erupted in which 12 policemen were killed and another 11 wounded in less than an hour, forcing the police to retreat.

Within hours of the Metis victory at Duck Lake, local Cree with grievances of their own began raiding stores and farms for arms, ammunition and food supplies while civilians fled. On March 28, when news reached the settlers at Battleford that several Native bands were headed in their direction, the town erupted in panic. Over the next two days, the entire population fled across the unstable ice bridge over the frozen Battle River, abandoning all their worldly possessions for the safety of nearby Fort Battleford. Over 500 civilians had taken refuge in the fort, protected by the palisade and 25 policemen commanded by Colonel Morris.

On March 30, Cree Chief Poundmaker asked for a meeting with Indian agent J.M. Rae. After Rae refused to meet with him, the Natives—many of whom were women seeking to feed their starving children—pillaged Battleford's abandoned homes and businesses for food and supplies. Warriors, unrestrained by Poundmaker, then put many buildings to the torch. When the Natives returned to Poundmaker's reserve a few days later, they left in their wake an eerily silent town, robbed of its riches and shrouded in smoke, but the huddled masses in Fort Battleford breathed a sigh of relief. Their lives had been spared, at least for now.

The same couldn't be said for the hamlet of Frog Lake, to the northwest of Battleford. On April 2, Cree warriors under Wandering Spirit descended on the community with a vengeance, massacring nine settlers before pillaging their homes.

On May 2, soldiers under Colonel Otter attacked Poundmaker's camp at Cut Knife Creek but were repulsed after a short firefight. The defeated troops fled headlong to Battleford and sought shelter at the NWMP fort. To Poundmaker's credit, he didn't allow his warriors to attack the fleeing troops, almost certainly preventing a massacre of the panicked, disorganized soldiers. However, on May 14, a wagon train carrying supplies for Colonel Otter was captured at Eagle Hills by a Native band.

But the tide was turning against the Metis and First Nations. Over four days from May 9 to May 12, 300 Metis and First Nations warriors were soundly defeated by 800 government troops at the Battle of Batoche. The Metis leader, Louis Riel, surrendered to British Major General Frederick Middleton on May 15. Less than two weeks later, with his allies having thrown in the white towel, Poundmaker was compelled to surrender at Fort Battleford on May 26.

The short-lived rebellion was over, but sadly not the killing. In the aftermath of the conflict, the largest mass hanging in Canada was held at Fort Battleford when eight First Nations men were hanged for their role in the Frog Lake Massacre. When they were cut down from the gallows they were buried just metres away. Their bodies remain there still, their graves marked by teepee poles. The tragedy of these events forms a noose around the spirits of the eight condemned men, tying them to our world when the natural order suggests they should have crossed over to the afterlife.

Today, Fort Battleford has a well-deserved reputation as one of the most haunted locations in Saskatchewan. What, exactly, makes it so haunted? People report hearing all manner of strange noises in and around the fort, including disembodied voices, spectral footsteps and, most ominously, Native war cries that send chills down the spine just as they would have done to the settlers more than a century ago. Objects move about on their own as if being manipulated by unseen hands. Spots so cold they lead to frosted breath even on the hottest of summer days suddenly materialize. And then there are the ghosts that crawl forth from their graves to terrify the living.

As one would expect, the area around the graves of the eight condemned men is a spectral hot spot. The mass hanging, an emotionally charged event, made a post-mortem imprint on the soil. There are recurring reports of people standing near the teepee poles that mark these graves hearing soft Native chanting on an otherwise still day. "I've heard it on more than one occasion," says a Battleford resident named Beth who has an interest in paranormal investigation. "The singing, or chanting, is clearly in a Native tongue. I keep thinking it's some sort of feedback loop from when the Natives were hanged here. Maybe it's the eight men singing quietly in the moments before they dropped to their deaths. Or maybe it's loved ones who mourned the dead as they hung at the end of the ropes. But who knows?"

To the surprise of many, though, the area around the gravesite of these condemned Native men isn't the most haunted location within the palisade of Fort Battleford—far from it. Instead, it's the officers' quarters, a building as creepy as it is historic, that's supposedly the most spiritually active. Within this structure, the paranormal is so common that it's almost, by definition, normal.

The resident apparition is that of the fort's assistant-surgeon. You may not find his story in history texts like you would that of those responsible for the Frog Lake Massacre, but it's no less tragic.

According to lore, the assistant-surgeon watched from the fort's palisades with growing fear as panicked settlers poured across the frozen Battle River and streamed into the fort on March 28, 1885, seeking shelter behind its walls from the raiding Natives. When smoke began to rise above the homes and businesses put to the torch by these Natives, the physician's terror reached new heights. He was certain the warriors would turn their attention to the fort next, and he knew that the only thing preventing them from pouring over the walls and venting their frustration on every white man sheltered there was a handful of NWMP constables.

Sleep eluded him. Those few moments when he nodded off were plagued by nightmares filled with bloodthirsty Native warriors brutally murdering every living soul in the fort. He was petrified of dying under a Native attack, or worse, being tortured by half-starved warriors venting years of pent-up frustration on the garrison and settlers. Under the weight of his growing terror, the physician's mind snapped. He locked himself in the upstairs office in the officers' quarters, loaded a rifle, placed it to his head and pulled the trigger.

That's the story as popularly told. Unfortunately, it is a myth. "The ghost in the officers' quarters is that of the fort's assistant-surgeon, that much is true. But the man died in 1887, not 1885—two full years after the rebellion. We know this for a fact; we actually have an unusually detailed account of his death and autopsy because the coroner, Mr. P.G. Laurie, was also the publisher of the *Saskatchewan Herald*," explains Conley-Blais, who notes that there's also serious doubt about how he died. Was it suicide or murder?

According to the newspaper account, Dr. Robert Miller, the fort's assistant-surgeon, complained to mess waiter Adolphus Manseau of not feeling well and requested that a plate of soup be brought to his room. Manseau brought the dinner to Miller's quarters a short while later, but his raps on the door went unanswered. Upon opening the door, the mess waiter was aghast to find the doctor lying dead upon the bed. The fort's officers were summoned; their observations were reported in ghoulish detail by the paper:

> Lying on his back upon the bed, with his outer clothes removed, covered with the bed clothes except his right foot, from which the stocking was removed, was all that remained of one who had so recently been mixing in their company. Upon the outside of the bed was a Snider rifle with the muzzle pointing towards the head of the bed, the barrel grasped tightly with both hands, held firmly in the rigor of death. Where the head should have been was but a confused and bloody mess, while scattered over the bed and the room were the fragments of skull and bone. On the floor at a distance of five or six feet from the bed lay one of the lobes of the brain, and on the dressing table the other, both unbroken. The condition of the walls at the head and back of the bed and of the room generally attested the violence of the explosion that had wrought the sad deed.

A verdict of suicide was quickly meted out. According to the officers, Miller had formed twine into a loop, one part of which he had securely fastened to the trigger while the other end was passed under the hollow of his foot. Placing the muzzle to his head or in his mouth, he straightened the leg and fired the gun, killing himself instantly.

It was open and shut. Or was it? When staff members at modern-day Fort Battleford began studying these reports, questions lingered. How did no one in the building, several of whom were assembled in the mess downstairs for dinner, hear the crack of the rifle as it fired? How could the rifle be "held firmly in the rigor of death" if, as the mess waiter reported, only a short time had passed between the time he was asked to prepare soup and the time he brought it to Miller's quarters? Why did Miller seem to be in the middle of undressing when he died? And perhaps most importantly, was it even possible to shoot oneself in the fashion described? Staff began to have their doubts.

"I've been here for 28 years. At first, when we would talk among ourselves about the assistant-surgeon's story, we referred to it as a suicide as the popular story went. At the time, the ghost was really active. I'd describe it as almost agitated. It was so bad that I refused to go into the officers' quarters by myself," says Conley-Blais. "Then we read the detailed autopsy report as published in the *Herald* and began questioning whether he did in fact commit suicide. It seems pretty clear he was likely murdered, and we began presenting the story as such. Since then, the ghost is not as agitated."

Regardless of exactly how he died, the assistant-surgeon did perish in the officers' quarters; his lifeblood soaked deep into the floorboards, binding his tormented spirit to the building. While most of the more dramatic ghost stories have taken place on the second floor where the gruesome death took place, the entirety of the officers' quarters crackles with spiritual energy, and one cannot be certain the surgeon's apparition won't manifest unexpectedly anywhere within the building.

Conley-Blais vividly recalls the experience of one visitor many years ago, back when the energy in the officers' quarters was particularly oppressive. "This woman, who had a really strong connection to spirits, walked into the building and immediately ran back out, really upset. She was hyperventilating and on the verge of passing out. When she was finally able to speak, she gave me a dire warning: 'Don't go in there; it's very dangerous.' It confirmed what I personally felt about the darkness of the energy in the building."

Even as the ghost has seemingly settled in recent years, poltergeist activity—the kind that leaves the witness questioning, 'Did I really just see that?'—commonly occurs in the officers' quarters. Objects have flown across rooms as if thrown by some invisible force, doors creak open by themselves, artifacts are playfully hidden, and inexplicable noises are heard. One visitor was startled when she felt a heavy hand on her shoulder—a hand she couldn't see.

The apparition of the assistant-surgeon has been seen on more than one occasion, typically in the form of a ghostly mist-like figure. Jillian remembers her experience in the building with emotion bordering on terror. She recalls the floorboards groaning under her shoes as she made her way through the various rooms. Jillian was walking down a hallway when a chill caressed the back of her neck—that inexplicable sense you get when something is off.

She stopped when she heard a voice behind her. Although the words were indistinguishable, like a mumbled whisper, it was a deep man's voice, ragged like that of a sick or old individual. She spun around; the hall was empty. "Hello? Is someone there?" Her heart raced as she waited for a reply. None came.

Jillian retraced her steps down the hall and tentatively peered into the first room, expecting to see a man. She was surprised to find the room empty.

Then she heard another deep whisper, again from behind her. Spinning again, Jillian's eyes grew wide as she watched a shadow, human-shaped but strangely elongated, sliding down the hall away from her. Long, dark fingers stretched out across the wall as if desperately reaching toward life and all that it once promised. With surprising speed the dark shape slid silently along the wall before blending in with the real shadows; then it was gone.

Horrified and suddenly chilled to the bone, Jillian ran. In some ways she's still running; the terror of that day haunts her dreams. A devout Catholic, she believes that the assistant-surgeon's suicide ensured the tragic soul wasted away into nothing but a shadow, a spirit trapped between realms and doomed to linger in the darkness.

Melissa Brown also had a frightening experience in the officers' quarters during her visit to Fort Battleford a few years back. While in the office upstairs, soaking in the environs and contemplating the history of the site, she heard a chair slide behind her as if someone was taking a seat at the desk. She turned to see who had joined her, but no one was there. Indeed, as she passed through the building on the way outside to where her husband was taking photographs, she saw no one in any of the rooms. She was all alone.

But that wasn't the end of her experience. As Melissa approached the exit, the door handle turned and rattled on its own as if someone was trying to open the door for her. An overwhelming chill consumed her. Was the spirit eager to be done with Melissa? Whether or not, it certainly hastened her exit.

To walk through Fort Battleford is like stepping back in time. Cannon fire echoes through the fort, and costumed staff tell stories of the settlement of the Canadian prairie as you wander the grounds and explore the buildings. The past may be closer at hand than staff or visitors expect, thanks to a number of souls that refuse to rest in death and who, on occasion, claw forth from their graves and prowl the fort in search of elusive peace.

See For Yourself

Fort Battleford was designated a National Historic Site of Canada in 1923 to commemorate its role in the 1885 Northwest Rebellion and, in a broader sense, in the settlement and development of the west. In 1951, the site became a national historic park, with many of the buildings restored or reconstructed for public visitation.

Today, Fort Battleford offers a glimpse into life in the late 1800s with the newly formed North-West Mounted Police (NWMP). Rent a headset at the visitor centre and take a self-guided audio tour, discovering 15 fact-filled spots around the fort and visiting five authentically restored buildings, from the grim prison to the more refined commanding officer's house. Along the way, uncover the central but little-known role of Fort Battleford in the conflict of 1885 and discover the stories of the NWMP, the Metis and First Nations people and the settlers in that troubled era.

Various special activities and events are held over the course of the May to August operating period. Every Canada Day, Fort Fest brings the fort alive with a huge, family-friendly event. Visitors can witness period tradesmen at work, see historic weapons and telegraph demonstrations, and watch NWMP horseback maneuvers while also enjoying modern entertainment, music and games.

Readers of this book will find the August lantern-lit ghost walks of particular interest. After the sun has dipped below the horizon, gather around the feeble light cast by the tour guide's lantern to hear stories of the restless ghosts that lurk in the shadowy recesses of the buildings on this historic site. "The only light comes from the lantern-bearer; otherwise it's pitch dark. The lack of light and the true ghost stories our staff share chill you to the bone and cause you look over your shoulder. It can be frightening, in the best possible way," enthuses Conley-Blais.

And then there is a much-anticipated Halloween event, where all five buildings are transformed into haunted houses with different themes. "I guarantee we'll make you scream," Conley-Blais laughs.

Whether you're interested in history or horror, Fort Battleford is an atmospheric site worthy of a visit.

Marie Dressler Museum: Spectre of a Hollywood Legend

~

Marie Dressler's image is grey and grainy. The heavy-set, aged movie star glides silently closer. The image flickers then skips entirely, causing Dressler to disappear from view for the blink of an eye. When she reappears, she is noticeably closer. Her smiling face suddenly turns serious. Her mouth moves as she speaks, but there is no sound. Whatever the actress is trying to say, the message is muted. It's impossible to comprehend the storyline. The image skips again and then goes black. Marie Dressler is gone.

But this is no grainy film from the vault of silent movies the actress starred in during her celebrated life. Instead, it's a real life experience from her childhood home in Cobourg, where Marie Dressler's filmy apparition has been seen for almost a century. Her spectral presence is part of the spectacle at the Marie Dressler Museum.

Although her story isn't exactly rags to riches, Marie Dressler (birth name Leila Koerber) was born in a modest, four-room cottage in Cobourg, Ontario, on November 9, 1868, and died 66 years later in an opulent mansion in Hollywood. She rose from simple beginnings to become one of the wealthiest film stars of her era and the first Canadian to grace the cover of *TIME* magazine. Despite her fortune and fame at the time of her death, Marie Dressler is far from a household name today.

In 1882, a starry-eyed 14-year-old Dressler wrote a letter to the Nevada Traveling Stock Company requesting a job. She knew from a young age that she wanted to devote her life to entertaining people, and she dreamt of becoming an accomplished Broadway actress in New York. Vaudeville was the first step in fulfilling her ambitions. It was at this time that she changed her name from Leila Koerber to save her family the embarrassment of having a daughter in show business, which at that time was a somewhat disreputable career.

Over the next couple of decades she worked in numerous vaudeville and stage productions, during which she perfected her acting and comedic skills and created the endeavouring, light-hearted persona that would later make her famous. Dressler's big break came when producer George Lederer cast her in a supporting role opposite Lillian Russell in *Princess Nicotine*. While she had a steady and successful stage career on Broadway and in London's West End, Dressler's real fame resulted from her work in film. She made the jump to movies in 1914 when she was cast alongside Charlie Chaplin in the silent film *Tillie's Punctured Romance*, and she made a string of movies thereafter.

It wasn't a smooth ride for Dressler in Hollywood; nothing about her career was easy. Throughout the 1920s she endured a slump and found so little work that she was virtually out of film. Depression pushed her to the edge of suicide, but her characteristic determination and resolve saw her through to a late-life career resurgence. Dressler reached her height of fame in the early 1930s, as a 60-something, 200-pound, undeniably plain woman.

In 1931, Marie won the Academy Award for Best Actress for her role as Min in the hit comedy film *Min and Bill*, and two years later, in the wake of her landmark role in the film *Tugboat Annie*, got the cover of *TIME* magazine. She was one of the highest-earning film stars of the day and indeed was a bigger box office draw than any of the other three MGM leading ladies of the era—Greta Garbo, Norma Shearer and Joan Crawford—who, in contrast to Dressler, have retained their fame through the decades.

Marie Dressler was one of the most beloved performers in America at her death from cancer on July 28, 1934. It was a shocking loss that left her fans grief stricken. The untimely nature of her death is possibly what has caused Marie Dressler's spirit to be so restless.

After her passing, an adoring public took renewed interest in Dressler's life and the modest Cobourg home in which was born. It was still a private residence in 1934, but then-owner Frederick Field decided to capitalize on this public interest by transforming the house into a fine-dining restaurant. When it opened in 1937, Dressler's many loyal fans jumped at the chance to visit her childhood home, ensuring the restaurant was an immediate success even as the Depression continued to grip the nation.

In fact, the restaurant became something of a tourist attraction. In those days, Cobourg's busy harbour owed a good part of its hubbub to wealthy Americans who made summer homes for themselves in what was then a quaint, idyllic town. Several steamers sailing daily from Rochester, New York, brought summer residents and tourists to town, and the birth-place of the star of *Tugboat Annie* was an irresistible draw.

The restaurant remained in the Field family until 1974, after which it changed hands a couple of times and then was painstakingly restored to make the rooms historically correct to the 1860s, when Marie Dressler was born. Sadly, on January 15, 1989, a fire ravaged the building. Now just a fire-blackened shell, its future was very much in doubt.

Recognizing the historic significance of the building, then-Cobourg and District Chamber of Commerce director Bill Patchett led a fundraising campaign to save Dressler's home and helped found the Marie Dressler Foundation. The efforts were successful, and the home was purchased, rebuilt, restored and transformed into the new home of the Chamber of Commerce. Today, the building is owned by the town of Cobourg and operates as the town's visitor information office and, since 2016, is home to the Marie Dressler Museum, devoted to the life and films of the actress.

It's to this home that Marie Dressler's spirit returned almost immediately after her death. Indeed, a number of guests and staff in the 1930s and 1940s spoke of seeing a filmy apparition resembling the recently-deceased screen idol in the newly opened restaurant. It was said the ghost most often materialized at the back of the restaurant before floating through the dining room and out through the front door. Perhaps she was attempting to leave; it's a sad truth that Marie Dressler is trapped in a place she fled as a teen to escape the abuse of her father. In a way, her childhood home is a form of prison to her spirit.

Sometimes Dressler would try to speak, but no sound would come out. It was like a scene from one of her silent movies. Witnesses strained to hear, but no matter how hard they tried, they could never make out any words; without the benefit of subtitles, her message was incomprehensible. When she grew frustrated, she would disappear. What was she trying so desperately to say?

One unusual aspect of this haunting is the anecdote about the phantom aroma of freshly brewed coffee wafting through the restaurant even when no coffee was being made. Did Dressler just like a good cup of coffee?

Another story dates back to the early 1980s, when Dressler's home was still a restaurant. "Carol" spent several months waiting tables to put her through university. Despite long hours that left her feet aching, she enjoyed the experience. Or at least she did until one October day.

Carol recalls crunching through fallen leaves as she walked up to the modest cottage and feeling an unusual presence as she reached for the door. It was almost as if something was putting up a barrier in an attempt to keep her out. She had never felt anything unnatural in the building, so she pushed the thought aside and stepped inside. There was a long, sad sigh. Carol heard it right in front of her, but she was alone. Then she felt unseen hands push her back to the door, which swept open with a cold gust of autumn air.

Startled, she jerked away from the invisible grip. "I'm leaving," she instinctively blurted out as she stepped out into the October chill. Swallowing hard, Carol stared wide-eyed at the door. Fear bubbled up within her. She then turned and left, cancelling her shift that day and working only a handful more days after that before quitting. She never again felt comfortable in the restaurant.

In more recent years, visitors to the museum have felt gusts of cold wind even though all the windows are shut. Others have felt someone watching them. Several people passing by the Marie Dressler Museum reported seeing a large woman peering out onto the street from the windows late at night. Shadows cast by streetlights can play tricks on the eye, but how does one explain how so people with no familiarity with the obscure actress—which would include all but the most rabid of classic film fans—have accurately described her?

The staff at the Cobourg Visitor Information Centre and Marie Dressler Museum seem reluctant to speak on the subject of ghosts. Is that because they don't want to draw any paranormal attention to the historic building? Or perhaps Marie Dressler's museum really is no longer home to her spirit, and the silent movie star is now enjoying her eternal reward. After all, she certainly worked hard enough during her Hollywood career to deserve a peaceful respite in death. Even if she has moved on, the performance of Marie Dressler's spirit over the years has ensured her a continued leading role in Cobourg's fright-filled folklore.

See For Yourself

Marie Dressler's near two-century-old home (built in 1833) is shared by the Cobourg Visitor Information Centre and the Marie Dressler Museum, each of which occupies half of the house.

The heart of the museum is the exhibit "From Cobourg to Hollywood: the Story of Marie Dressler," which traces her life from its humble beginnings to the height of her fame and fortune in the film industry. For more than 25 years, the Marie

Dressler Foundation has made a dedicated effort to assemble a historical collection to chronicle the story of Dressler's life and career. Visitors to the museum admire a number of artifacts from this impressive collection, which include photographs, print ephemera, newsreel clips and movies, in so doing becoming familiar—likely for the first time—with a largely forgotten but highly influential Hollywood star.

A Beacon of Spectral Activity: West Point Lighthouse Inn and Museum

~

Carol Livingstone has lived within sight of Prince Edward Island's West Point Lighthouse all her 74 years and has an unusual affinity to the majestic tower. Her grandfather, Lighthouse Willie, was the first and longest-serving keeper; as a child, she and her friends would head over to the tower to be regaled with stories by then-keeper Benny MacIsaac, who never failed to let them climb the stairs to the light and climb out onto the ring around it; and as a teenager and dating, the light served as a nightlight of sorts, reminding her that when she saw its beam turn on, it was time to return home. Many years later, Carol was instrumental in turning the lighthouse into a museum to preserve local heritage.

Few people know the West Point Lighthouse as well as Carol, and fewer still love it with greater passion. That's why, when she asserts the building is haunted—and has stories to back up her claims—you're forced to take heed.

"When I was a child I heard all kinds of stories about the lighthouse and the area, including tales of ghost ships, buried treasure, sea serpents…When the lighthouse opened as a museum, I had some strange experiences of my own in the building that just couldn't be explained. I don't have any doubt the lighthouse is haunted," she says. "One event occurred when I was working late in the tower. I was in one of the bedrooms, folding and pricing t-shirts for the gift shop. At a quarter to twelve, the built-in light above the bed suddenly went out. I took it as a hint it was time to go bed. I crawled under the blankets, and at half past two, that light came back on by itself. It was spooky because there was no explanation—the rest of the lights in the lighthouse were working fine, so it wasn't a power outage or electrical problem."

West Point Lighthouse has a number of distinctions that set it apart from other lighthouses on Prince Edward Island. At a height of 21 metres, it is the tallest square-based lighthouse on PEI. On a clear day, from the top you can make out New Brunswick across the Northumberland Strait. Built in 1875–76, it's also one of the oldest lighthouses in the province and the first one built after PEI entered Confederation in 1873. And, if you

The West Point Lighthouse is the tallest and most haunted lighthouse on the island.

believe the many stories over the years, West Point Lighthouse is the most haunted lighthouse on Prince Edward Island, perhaps even in all of Canada.

Building the lighthouse was an engineering and logistical challenge. The foundation was built atop a cribwork of logs to distribute the weight and keep it from sinking into the sand. Because there was no building stone available on the island, rocks for the foundation had to be imported by schooner from Nova Scotia. To ballast the tower and provide stability, large rocks were placed inside the thick walls of the first storey. The first two floors of the tower served as an extension of the attached one-and-a-half-storey keeper's dwelling; the tower's bottom floor was used as a parlour, and the second floor was divided into two bedrooms. Completed in less than a year, West Point Lighthouse began operation on May 21, 1876.

Incredibly, only two keepers tended the lighthouse during the 88 years before it became electric and automated. The first lighthouse keeper was William "Lighthouse Willie" Mac-Donald. He and his wife Mariah owned a farm 3 kilometres from the lighthouse. During winter, the MacDonald family, which steadily grew to include eight children, lived on the farm, but as soon as the ice melted, heralding the opening of sea navigation, the family would move to the lighthouse. MacDonald served at West Point Lighthouse for 50 years, and upon his retirement in 1925, was awarded an Imperial Long Service Medal for his dedication on behalf of Britain's King George V.

The next, and final, lighthouse keeper was Benjamin MacIsaac, a local farmer who served and was wounded in France during World War I. Because his family consisted of 15 children, Benjamin and his wife, Pearl, never resided in the keeper's house, instead living year-round on their farm a few kilometres away. Every evening during the navigation season, MacIsaac would hike over to the lighthouse and spend the night tending to the light. West Point Lighthouse was automated on May 19, 1963, forcing MacIsaac's retirement after 38 years of service.

But that wasn't the end of the lighthouse's story. In 1983, work began to transform the lighthouse into a museum and inn. The dwelling was renovated using the original blueprints. On

The West Point Lighthouse is a unique attraction on Prince Edward Island as a museum/inn combination.

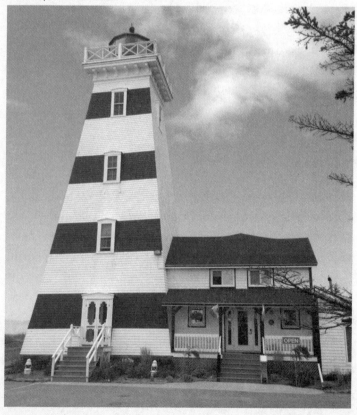

July 1, 1984, the new facility opened as what was then Canada's only inn located in a lighthouse, with visitors having the opportunity to stay in the same room that keeper Willie MacDonald reserved for guests. A few years later, a large addition was added to house additional guest rooms.

Sleeping in a lighthouse is memorable experience, made all the more authentic by the continued presence of original keeper Willie McDonald, whose apparition occasionally appears before startled guests after the sun has settled below the horizon. It's believed Willie didn't miss a single night during his tenure, not for sickness or for vacation. Willie's dedication to the lighthouse extends beyond the grave, a fact most guests find comforting rather than unsettling.

Many guests report that their bedroom's lights mysteriously turned on when no one else was around. That's nothing new. Willie has been playing around with the lights for decades. In the years immediately following the 1980s conversion to an inn and museum, it was routine for museum volunteers to spend a couple of nights each week in the lighthouse to give the manager time off. They would huddle inside and listen to the waves crashing and the wind buffeting the tower. To these volunteers, all of the sounds that might haunt the sleep of a guest were routine and entirely explainable. They were as in-tune with the lighthouse as anyone since the last keeper left in 1963. Yet there were many restless nights plagued by strange sounds and inexplicable sights in the tower.

One summer evening after the restaurant had closed and staff had left for the night, Merna Boulter, the volunteer on duty, was alone and impatiently watching the clock. If no guests had checked into the inn by 9:00 PM, she could lock up the lighthouse and go home. Fighting off boredom and the lure of sleep, Merna watched the clock slowly tick away the time. Finally, after what seemed like an eternity, the clock struck nine and she was free to leave. There was just one final chore to perform: climb the 72 steps to the top of the lighthouse to make sure all was well.

Up she went, one stair at a time; the only sound that accompanied her footsteps was the crashing of the waves on the beach outside. Once at the top, Merna took a quick peak around, found nothing amiss and retraced her steps down the tower. Satisfied all was well, she turned off the lights, locked the door behind her and got in her car.

Merna happened to glance in the rearview mirror as she was driving away and was stunned to see light coming from the bedroom above the lighthouse veranda. She knew every light had been turned off before she locked up; that was the point of her final inspection, after all. Confused and a little agitated that her return home was being delayed, Merna went back in to investigate. She climbed the stairs and entered the lit room. It was empty. There were no sounds; nothing stirred. Merna turned off the light and left once again.

Back in her car, Merna risked another glance back at the lighthouse. What she saw caused her heart to skip a beat: the light in that room was once again on. That was all the poor woman's frayed nerves could take. There was no way she was going back into the lighthouse that night. If a ghost wanted the light on that badly, she wasn't about to argue with it. Instead, she put the car into gear and headed for the safety and comfort of her home.

There was another, eerily similar episode a few years later. Carol Livingstone was among a group of volunteers who had stayed late going over an architect's plans for renovating the lighthouse's kitchen. Finally, well into the evening, exhaustion caught up with them and they decided to call it a day. Before locking up, they turned off all the switches on the main electrical control panel except—naturally—for the one that controlled the navigation light. They made absolute certain to take this measure because someone had broken in a short while before, slept in one of the bedrooms and left the electric heating on, resulting in an exorbitant heating bill.

Just as they piled into their car, Carol suddenly remembered that the architect's plans had been left on the kitchen table. She had to go back for them. Grabbing a flashlight, she raced back into the dark building. She neither saw nor heard anything amiss as she gathered the plans and then headed back to the car.

Driving home in the dark, they came upon a figure in the road waving his arms. They stopped the car and were told by the clearly upset man that a distraught and possibly suicidal neighbour was missing. West Point is a small, tight-knit community, so now the museum volunteers were concerned as well. What if the man decided to break into the lighthouse and end his life by flinging himself from the top?

Although she had locked the door, Carol and the other volunteers decided it would be best to return to the lighthouse and double check that the man had not found his way in. They didn't want a death on their conscience. Upon arriving, they found the front door still locked and secure. They began to breathe easier—at least until they entered and found the kitchen fully illuminated. How was this even possible? The control panel's switches were still turned off, so the lights were receiving no power. Yet in spite of all logic, the lights were indeed on. In the absence of any rational explanation, the volunteers were forced to accept what just a short while before they would have considered irrational: Willie was still on duty. (And for those readers who are concerned, the despondent man was found safe. He hadn't gone anywhere near the lighthouse.)

Carol relates more strange happenings. "I was alone in the lighthouse on another occasion. I was coming down the stairs from the third to the second floor and was passing a door that leads into a small bedroom. I happened to look over and see a man in front of the window. It looked just like Lighthouse Willie. I was shocked, as you can imagine," she said. "A couple of years later, in 1991, I was having a conversation with a writer from Louisiana in the lighthouse parlour. Out of the blue, she asked if I'd ever had an unusual experience in the lighthouse. She said that she had been all through the lighthouse and was pulled by a male presence to one specific spot—a spot right in front of the window in that bedroom where I saw Willie. She couldn't have known my story. It was eerie."

Not every ghost story tied to West Point relates to Willie, however. There's another, older story that casts a supernatural shadow over the area. With a ghost ship, bloodthirsty pirates, buried treasure and an ancient curse, it's one heck of a tale.

In the early 1800s, a farmer named John was plagued by a vivid nightmare that tormented his sleep for nights on end. He would thrash restlessly before waking suddenly, jolting up in bed with a wild look in his eyes and his heart pounding in his chest. The nightmare was terrifying in its realism.

In his dream, John sees a black pirate vessel crewed by hard-looking cutthroats sailing along the shore of Prince Edward Island. As the ship sails on, the high red cliffs give way to soft, sandy beaches, and one of the lookouts hollers, "There's a cove ahead, Cap'n Kidd."

The notorious pirate, Kidd, appears on deck, his appearance as fearsome as his reputation. "We're goin' in, me hearties," he commands, "fer if the King's men catch us with this load, we'll hang from the yardarm."

The ship sails into the cove and then drops anchor. Captain Kidd and a boy of about 15 come ashore in a rowboat. Kidd hefts a large chest onto his shoulder as he strides toward the sand dunes just inland with the scrawny lad following behind, shovel in hand. In the shadow of three trees, the boy is commanded to dig a hole in the ground deep enough to accommodate the treasure chest. The chest is dropped into the hole and buried. Then Kidd grabs the exhausted boy, drags him to the nearest tree and ties him there. "Watch the treasure, lad, and anyone who tries to take it before I come back will die fer their greed."

Kidd then leaves the boy there to die, ignoring the begging and pleading as he rows out to his ship.

John would wake from the dream, drenched in sweat and on the verge of tears for the boy who was so cruelly left to die. One night the boy's ghost appeared before John. Perhaps anticipating that the farmer would go hunting for the buried treasure, the wavering apparition warned John that he must dig only under the light of the moon and that no one could utter a word while they were recovering it, or a deadly curse would be placed upon them all.

Just as the ghost predicted, John came down with treasure fever. He was convinced his dream was a glimpse into the past. John shared the nightmare with some neighbours, and they agreed to help him search for the treasure. One day, they climbed into a boat and sailed around the island, looking for the distinctive cove John saw in his dream. They came upon the gently sloping sand dunes of West Point, and there it was—the very scene John had seen in his dream.

The men were excited, but heeding the ghost's warning, they waited until darkness fell to begin their search. As the mist rolled in from the sea, they began to dig in silence. Not long after, there was the dull thud of shovels hitting a solid oak chest.

Reflexively, someone cried out in excitement. In that split second, the curse was called down upon the diggers. Like a tidal wave, the excavated sand poured back into the hole, threatening to bury the men with the treasure chest. Scrambling for their lives, they barely crawled out of the hole before it filled back in. From the cove came the sound of anchor chains being hoisted. The men rushed to the shore in time to see a black pirate ship put out to sea and to hear a hoarse voice float back across the waves say, "You've guarded me treasure well, boy." Grateful to have survived and not willing to risk their lives any further, none of the men ever again attempted to claim Kidd's buried treasure.

Others have. In fact, so many tried that at one point in the late 19th century the dunes around the West Point Lighthouse were a moonscape of holes. The curse promised death to those who attempted to steal Kidd's treasure, and several treasure hunters did die suddenly and somewhat mysteriously. One healthy young man caught pneumonia and died almost immediately after digging, while another fell from a roof and was killed.

Does the ghostly boy still guard a cursed treasure in the shadow of the West Point Lighthouse? Many believe so. But thankfully the curse extends no farther than the pit in which the horde is hidden. The lighthouse itself is free of such darkness; its resident spirit, Lighthouse Willie, remains out of a sense of duty rather than any cursed compulsion, and as such is a benevolent, comforting presence. Care to spend a night and see for yourself?

See For Yourself

West Point Lighthouse Inn and Museum is unique in being both a comfortable inn and a museum wherein guests can explore Prince Edward Island's rich coastal history. It may lack the amenities and frills of larger hotels, but when it comes to pure aesthetic appeal, West Point Lighthouse Inn and Museum may well be PEI's most impressive place to rest your head. Enjoy spectacular sunsets and drift off to the sound of gently rolling waves from one of 13 guest rooms, each offering breathtaking views out onto the Northumberland Strait. If you truly want to get into the "spirit" of the place, stay in the Keeper's Quarters or the Tower Room, both located in the historic tower itself.

The museum is just as impressive. Home to PEI's most complete collection of lighthouse artifacts, memorabilia and exhibits, it tells the story of the West Point Lighthouse and its keepers, the local community (to whose continued passion the museum owes its existence) and the history of PEI's many maritime beacons. The tiny province has a long and proud maritime history that deserves to be preserved and recognized. The West Point Lighthouse—a wistfully beautiful maritime relic from the Victorian era—does just that.

Natural heritage is near at hand as well. Trails marked with interpretive signs meander through West Point's varied ecosystem of beaches, dunes and wooded areas. From these you can experience the best of Prince Edward Island.

Enduring Mysteries and Eerie Encounters at the Billy Bishop Home and Museum

~

Brianna saw the girl as she stood in the open doorway of a second-floor bedroom. She stared at the girl, who looked to be about her own age, seven years old. She was freckled, with large dark eyes and brown hair that reached past her shoulders. She wore a long, yellow dress and sat on the edge of a bed, swinging her legs, smiling sweetly.

She raised a finger to her lips. "Shhhhh." Then she giggled softly and disappeared.

Brianna gave a startled cry and stepped back from the room, then ran off to find her parents.

A while later, when the family was leaving the Billy Bishop Home and Museum, Brianna glanced over her shoulder for one last look at the elegant Victorian-era house. She gasped. Way down the hall, the mysterious girl poked her head out of a room. She waved goodbye, a big grin on her face.

More than a decade later, Brianna still remembers that day. Hers is just one of many unforgettable encounters reported by visitors to Billy Bishop's boyhood home in Owen Sound.

Billy Bishop. The name rings down through the decades, his exploits and heroism eternal. The most famous of hundreds of thousands of young Canadian men who served during World War I was Billy Bishop, Canada's top flying ace with 72 victories. He was a legend, a Victoria Cross recipient who represented the romance of flying and the supposed chivalry of air-to-air combat between modern-day cavaliers of the sky.

Readers avidly followed his exploits in newspapers and devoured his 1918 book, *Winged Warfare.* There wasn't a young boy in Canada at the time who couldn't recount Bishop's most famous exploit, the action of June 2, 1917. Early that morning, he flew alone over German lines deep into enemy territory to attack a heavily defended airfield, strafing the planes lined up on the runway before shooting down three German fighters sent up to intercept him. Bishop's action was daring, courageous and unprecedented. It earned him the Victoria Cross. Billy Bishop was a hero larger than life.

William Avery Bishop Jr. had a modest background with nothing to suggest the fame that would come his way. He was born in Owen Sound in 1894 to William Bishop Sr., a lawyer and the county registrar, and his wife, Margaret Greene. Billy and his siblings—older brother, Worth, and younger sister, Louise—grew up in the comfortable home at 948 3rd Avenue West that his father had built in 1882. He grew up an avid outdoorsman who enjoyed riding and swimming, and he became an excellent shot, which would benefit him later as a fighter pilot. The only hint of what the future held in store for the young Billy was his interest in the infant field of aviation. As a boy, Bishop crafted his own flying machine from a crate and bed sheets, which he launched from the roof of the house only for it to land in his mother's rose bushes below.

In 1911, at the age of 17, Billy Bishop enrolled at the Royal Military College in Kingston. When World War I erupted in 1914, the senior cadet resigned from school and enlisted in the army; he was posted to the cavalry and departed for Europe in June 1915.

A month later, his boyhood passion for flying was reignited when Bishop saw an airplane land in a nearby field. He immediately applied for a transfer to the Royal Flying Corps and, after months as an observer and months more of flight training, was sent to the front lines as a fighter pilot in March 1917. Bishop was a natural, perhaps more at home in a cockpit than he was on land. Less than two months later, Bishop had already recorded 22 aerial victories. Not all his successes that year were military; in October, Billy Bishop wed Margaret Burden, a woman with who he would share the rest of his life.

In 1918, the now-famous pilot was promoted and named Commander of No. 85 Squadron, nicknamed the Flying Foxes. Over the next few months he brought his total victories to 67 enemy aircraft. On June 19, his final day in France, Bishop shot down five German airplanes in 12 minutes to bring his victories to 72, more than any other Canadian during the war.

Billy Bishop transitioned uneasily to peace. He and fellow Canadian ace William Barker attempted the creation of an airline, Bishop-Barker Aeroplanes Limited, to provide passenger service from Toronto to Muskoka, but it failed after a few short seasons. Eventually, he found success in business.

But he never left his passion for aviation, nor his legend as a flying ace, completely behind. In 1936, Bishop was made an honorary Air Vice-Marshall, from which position he advocated for more funds and expansion of the Royal Canadian Air Force in the face of a looming war with Nazi Germany. During World War II, Bishop became Director of Recruiting for the RCAF, keeping up a hectic schedule travelling the country to ensure that a steady flow of young men stepped forward to serve King and Country. He also found time to pen his second book, *Winged Peace*, published in 1944, which contained his views on the future of aviation.

Bishop lived long enough to see the dawn of the jet age, dying in his sleep on September 11, 1956. His death was reported around the world, and Bishop was given a military funeral at Timothy Eaton Memorial Church in Toronto. Twenty-five thousand people lined the funeral procession route. Even today, with World War I a century in the past, Billy Bishop remains celebrated and remembered in Canada. He's among the front ranks of Canada's lexicon of heroes.

As a result of his legendary achievements, Bishop's boyhood home in Owen Sound was named a National Historic Site and has become one of the community's most popular tourist destinations. Many people believe it is also thoroughly haunted. Visitors will occasionally feel something unusual, a distinct but intangible sense of someone unseen watching them. The person may see movement out of the corner of his eye, perhaps even catch a momentary glimpse of a figure, and yet he's completely alone in the room. The individual is left shaking. A trick of the light? Maybe. Or perhaps something else—something unexplainable.

Sometimes, if you listen carefully, disembodied footsteps can he heard. They sound decisive and heavy, like a man's footsteps, and it's believed that Billy Bishop himself may have returned home—either by choice or through spiritual connection to one of his belongings that are exhibited in the museum. One woman would feel an icy cold spot every time she got to a certain step on the staircase leading to the second floor. The chill, which she described as being so intense that it would cut to the bone, was limited to this single step. Climb one stair higher or step back one, and the cold would instantly dissipate. There is no explanation.

Poltergeist-like activity often leaves staff scratching their heads. Many are not believers in ghosts or the paranormal before they come to work at the National Historic Site but are converted when they witness things that cannot be explained—such as a knife that moves across the kitchen by itself, a door that repeatedly closes by itself overnight or artifacts that simply fall off shelves before a startled witness. Most of these incidents are playful rather than frightening, but they leave no doubt that the Billy Bishop Home and Museum is indeed haunted. Not everyone takes this knowledge well; some staff members are so unnerved by these experiences that they are uncomfortable working at the museum alone.

Although it's generally assumed the spirits inhabiting the Billy Bishop Home are benevolent, sometimes when the worlds of the living and the dead collide unexpectedly, terrifying things occur. For example, students are invited to set up their own exhibits in a display area in the kitchen. One teenaged girl was working on a display when she saw a shadow emerge from a closed door. She was paralyzed with fear; her chin quivered, but nothing else moved. The black shadow floated silently across the room to another door and then disappeared from view by passing right through the door, leaving in its wake a cold that goose-pimpled the teenager's skin and numbed her nose. She raced from the building. It took her several days to wrap her head around what she saw and to summon the courage to return to the museum to complete her exhibit.

During a veterans' commemoration event, a woman named Jackie was alone on the second floor when she heard a male voice behind her. She spun around, startled, but no one was there—no one human, at least. She was especially mystified because this was not just some lost ghost wandering the halls—whatever it was actually called her by name.

Psychics have sensed Bishop's presence, and several people have claimed to see the old aviator's ethereal silhouette over the years. Maybe it shouldn't be a surprise that Bishop's ghost haunts his childhood home. After all, he was a man of willpower and courage. If anyone should defy the call of death, it would be Billy Bishop.

Despite his fame and larger-than-life stature, Billy Bishop's spirit is not the one most widely encountered in the museum. Instead, that honour falls to a seemingly insignificant young girl, a child who couldn't have lived long enough to leave her mark in the world. Yet she is the most celebrated ghost within the walls of the Billy Bishop Home and Museum, perhaps in all of Owen Sound.

Over the years, staff and visitors alike have reported seeing this little girl in a pretty Victorian dress. Often she is seen out of the corner of the eye but disappears when that person tries to look directly at her. Other times, she stands before witnesses looking as real as you or me and may be mistaken for a costumed interpreter except for the startling suddenness of her disappearance. Occasionally, she appears to only one person in a crowded room, leaving the sole witness to question his sanity.

Ghost stories were very much a holiday tradition in the 19th century, as much a part of the season as a roast goose on the table or stockings hung by the fire with care. In the evening, families would gather around a fire crackling in the hearth to share chilling tales. It may seem unusual to us today, but it made sense to people in the past. When the night grows long and the year is coming to a close, it's only natural for people to huddle together and to remember people and places of the past. The most enduring example of this tradition is Charles Dickens' *A Christmas Carol*, but there were in fact many more (including another by Dickens that centred around a grave robber being abducted by goblins on Christmas Eve to demonstrate the error of his ways).

No Victorian yuletide season was complete without a scary ghost story, so it perhaps makes an eerie sort of sense that at least one person should experience a frightening true ghost story during the Billy Bishop museum's annual Victorian Christmas event. It just wouldn't be an authentic Victorian Christmas otherwise.

The event is full of nostalgic warmth. The entire home is decorated in traditional fashion, with a bushy wreath on the front door, big bows on the tree in the parlour and garland draping the mantles and banisters. Carols are sung and Father Christmas makes a visit, allowing children the chance to plead their case to be placed on the Nice list. It's the most cherished date on the museum's calendar.

One gentleman man who participated in the Victorian Christmas event in 2001 experienced something slightly different. He was thoroughly enjoying himself, soaking up the old-fashioned charm and reflecting back on simpler Christmases of his youth when he entered the pantry and, out of the corner of his eye, saw a little girl dressed appropriately to the 19th century. He was momentarily startled because he thought he was alone. When he turned his head to look directly at her, the girl had disappeared.

The man was terrified. His stomach clenched into a tight knot. He raced from the pantry and ran into Mary Smith, the museum's manager at the time. Mary could see he was in shock. She asked what was wrong, and in a shaky voice the man related the shocking tale. Though a skeptic herself, Mary believed him—he was too frightened, the emotions he displayed too raw, for it to be anything but the truth. The man had wanted an authentic Victorian Christmas experience. He had gotten one, ghost and all.

Then there was another incident a few years later, when a man and his wife visited the museum. The couple began exploring the historic home, thoroughly enjoying themselves. Not long after arriving, they stepped into the home's kitchen. The man's eyes swept around the room, taking in his surroundings before they settled on a mannequin dressed up in the style of a period maid. A young girl in a frilly dress, aged perhaps five or six, stood partially behind the figure, peeking out from behind its apron with big brown eyes and a warm smile. The girl was clearly shy, but she smiled again when the man waved at her. Then he turned away and went about his exploration, thinking nothing of the meeting. Later, however, it would trouble his thoughts.

Sometime afterwards, while he and his wife reflected on their afternoon at the museum, he asked what she thought of the little girl in the kitchen: "Wasn't she cute as a button, in her old-fashioned dress?" Incredibly, his wife hadn't seen the girl. The man was shocked; how could she not? The girl was right there. Yet his wife was adamant; she hadn't seen a young girl, not in the kitchen or anywhere else. The man was now completely unnerved. Had his wife somehow simply missed the girl, or had he made eye contact with and waved at an apparition?

The question left him restless for a number of days thereafter, plaguing his dreams at night and troubling his thoughts throughout the day. Finally, in an effort to make sense of the affair, he returned to the Billy Bishop museum and asked Mary Smith if there had been a little girl in a costume there during his earlier visit.

The manager was taken aback. There hadn't been any young girls matching that description at the museum that day, neither a staff member's child nor a visitor. She had no explanation and could do nothing to salve the man's frayed nerves. The only conclusion either one could make was that the girl was, as the man had feared, the ghost of a child long dead.

The identity of this apparition is a perplexing, nagging mystery that has yet to be solved. Staff members at the Billy Bishop Home and Museum don't know of any young girls dying in the house during its 125-year history. Is the spirit that of someone with a more tenuous, but nonetheless intimate, connection to the home, perhaps that of an extended family member?

There's another possibility, however, one put forth by Mary Smith after the ghost investigations brought renewed attention to the local lore associated with the building. She reminds us that Billy had another older brother, Kilbourn, who died in 1892, before Billy was born. Kilbourn was seven years old when he died, likely of tuberculosis, and likely within the home. Smith made the point that young children's clothes in Victorian times may look feminine to a modern observer, and the ghost girl could be a boy. Could so many people be wrong? I think it unlikely, but who knows for sure.

In an effort to reveal some of the mysteries surrounding the resident ghost, staff called in Jeff Ostrander, a Barrie-based paranormal researcher who, over the past decade or so, has conducted investigations in a number of locations across Simcoe County and surrounding environs, ranging from Inn at the Falls in Muskoka to Museum on the Boyne in Alliston. He's a respected voice in the community, and having witnessed one of his investigations first hand, I can attest to the cautious, thorough and rational approach Ostrander takes to his work.

He brought that approach to the Billy Bishop Home and Museum during two separate investigations. In both cases, Ostrander's team was alone in the building, conducting their experiments from 8:00 PM to 2:00 AM with the assistance of a trusted psychic.

Ostrander begins by determining if there is a logical explanation for supposed paranormal phenomena. Perhaps the ghost-like fluttering of drapery is caused by blasts of air from a nearby vent, or maybe eerie orbs are nothing more than outside lights reflected through a window. The investigation at the Billy Bishop house began in this way, mapping and photographing the building to identify the location of windows, vents, wiring and other fixtures that might influence one's experiences and also affect the investigator's own instruments. Ostrander found nothing that could directly explain away any of the unusual experiences reported by staff and guests over the years.

Equipped with the full range of tape recorder, video surveillance and heat sensors, Ostrander and team hoped to detect the presence of spirits and perhaps even determine their identities and why they linger after their natural time on earth has drawn to a close. Some fascinating findings emerged.

A number of haunting sounds—electronic voice phenomena (EVPs)—come across clearly on tape recordings, and yet were not heard by the investigators at the time. For example, upon playing back the recordings, eerie grumblings—like those of an angry, incoherent man—took the investigators aback. Although used to all manner of unusual phenomena, several members of the team admitted that a cold shiver ran down their spines when they heard this inexplicable sound.

There were also ghostly yells that had no origin. Picked up in the museum's education room, the voice is clearly that of a male spirit. His words can't quite be made out, but he seems to be saying "shot it" or perhaps "got it." Is this a spectral echo of Billy Bishop himself, reliving the adrenaline-filled moments of one of his aerial victories in World War I? Is he yelling to be heard above the whistling wind and the roaring of his plane's engine? It's possible.

Another recording captured a raspy male voice that seemed to be whispering, "Paula!" The voice is hushed, but there's some urgency to it. Museum manager Mary Smith, a noted skeptic on all things paranormal, was impressed by the clarity of the voice and was forced to concede the possibility that ghosts did indeed exist. "They (Jeff Ostrander and team) may make me into a believer. They've got my curiosity up," she admitted in a post-investigation interview.

Interestingly, just before this mysterious voice was captured, the psychic felt the presence of an unseen male figure within the room. He communicated to her that he was desperately searching for someone named Paula. His spirit faded too quickly for the psychic to ask any questions or gain further insight. It was only much later, during the post-investigation findings, that the psychic realized the team's equipment had also captured the spirit's search for Paula.

Is Paula the little girl who has taken up eternal residence within the Billy Bishop Home and Museum? Who was she in life, and how is connected to the Bishop home? Why does she so stubbornly remain? The questions nagged at Smith. She and other museum staff have done extensive research into the various inhabitants of the Bishop house over the years and have not found any evidence of anyone named Paula. There's one possibility, though: there is still a decade's worth of maids who have yet to be identified. Could Paula have been a maid or other household servant? Was Paula a dear friend of the Bishops', or maybe an extended family member? We just don't know.

The Billy Bishop home has been so faithfully restored and so lovingly preserved that museum staff may have unknowingly fuelled the paranormal energy of the past. Maybe ghosts feel comfortable in what are—to them, at least—familiar surroundings. In their minds it's home, so why should they leave?

Visiting the Billy Bishop Home and Museum is like stepping back in time, as if you've been extended a gracious invitation to visit the Bishop family for afternoon tea or a Christmas party. The front door opens and you're welcomed into their residence. Your visit lasts a few hours. But Billy Bishop, Canada's flying ace of aces, and an unnamed girl in a frilly dress never depart. The home is their ever-lasting sanctuary…or maybe it's their prison.

See For Yourself

Visit this beautiful Victorian house and museum in the heart of Owen Sound. Explore the lives of the Bishop family and rediscover the man behind a Canadian icon. Authentic Billy Bishop artifacts include the uniform, complete with insignia, that he wore as Air Marshall; the antique desk that occupied his office in Ottawa during World War II; a bookcase with school books used by young Billy and his sister, Louise; a Royal Military College yearbook with Billy's picture and biography; and a share in the Bishop-Barker Aeroplane Company, among others. Beyond merely focusing on Billy Bishop, the museum also serves to remember the contributions of the many service men and women from Owen Sound and region.

The Billy Bishop Home and Museum engages the community through a variety of seasonal programs and events. Highlights of the year include Billy's birthday on February 8; Victorian teas throughout the summer, where you experience some of the elegance and refinement of social gatherings of the day; and Honouring Our Local Veterans in the fall. Perhaps the most anticipated event is Victorian Christmas, where guests can experience the nostalgic charm of a 19th-century yuletide celebration.

A Gallery of Ghosts:
Burnaby Art Gallery

~

When the subject of haunted buildings in British Columbia comes up in conversation, one of the first locations to be mentioned is almost always Fairacres, a century-old mansion with a troubled and somewhat sordid past that is now home to the Burnaby Art Gallery.

In 1909, a wealthy and successful New York businessman by the name of Henry Tracy Ceperley moved to Burnaby, British Columbia, in search of tranquility and solitude to live out the balance of his life. He built a beautiful home for himself and his second wife, Grace, on the north shore of Deer Lake. Designed by the renowned British architect R.P.S. Twizell, Ceperley's manor reflected his wealth and flamboyant character. No expense was spared in building the three-storey, 32-room mansion. Ceperley insisted on having all the latest innovations, and furnishings were imported from across America and as far away as Europe. Features included a veranda across the eastern side with spectacular views of the mountains, a billiard room with a beamed ceiling and an inglenook fireplace, and an impressive dining room with crystal chandeliers and expensive chinaware. The grounds were equally lavish, complete with manicured lawns, formal gardens, greenhouses, water features, horse stables and sculpted hedges that looked out onto a lake— all of which led to the Ceperleys naming their estate Fairacres. At the time of its completion in 1911, there was no house in Burnaby that could match Fairacres' size and grandeur.

Grace Ceperley loved the gardens and spent most of her time outside, surrounded by the peacefulness of nature, the vibrancy of the flowers that she lovingly tended and the joyful songs of the wild birds that she faithfully fed. Grace also adored children. Although never blessed with children of her own, she lavished affection upon her stepchildren and grandchildren and was generous in her support of worthy youth causes.

When Grace died in 1917 at the age of 54, it was revealed that she—a woman of considerable means in her own right, thanks to a sizable bequest from her brother-in-law—was actually the sole owner of the mansion. She had willed Fairacres to Henry, but with the stipulation that if the property were ever sold the proceeds would be used to construct a children's playground in Vancouver's Stanley Park. Three years after Grace's passing, Henry sold Fairacres and moved to California, but he didn't immediately leave money for the construction of a park, as per Grace's dying wishes. In fact, the money came only years later, upon Henry's own death in 1929, aged 79.

We don't why Henry delayed. Some people have speculated it was out of some sort of spite, and that this flagrant ignoring of her dying wishes riled Grace's undead spirit into activity. However, this theory flies in the face of evidence that the couple were very much devoted to one another. Indeed, Henry's children adored their stepmother. We simply don't know why Henry delayed in bequeathing the money for the children's playground, and to speculate would be presumptuous and unfair.

Instead of becoming a beloved home again, Fairacres was eventually sold to the City of Vancouver and converted into a tuberculosis ward of the Vancouver General Hospital. Pain and suffering, worry and despair, death—the once-grand mansion became weighed down by negative emotion. In 1939, the tuberculosis ward was moved and Fairacres became the home of an order of Benedictine monks who were establishing a priory in British Columbia. Although their stay was relatively brief, they left a lasting legacy in the form of a large gymnasium that has since been converted into a theatre. Then, in 1954, the mansion changed hands yet again. A new religious order moved in, one whose beliefs were diametrically opposed to those of the Catholic friars.

Fairacres was now the sanctuary of a strange and malevolent cult known as the Temple of the More Abundant Life. Headed by William Franklin Wolsey, a charlatan who called himself Archbishop John I and who was wanted throughout the United States on a string of charges for bigamy, assault and extortion, the cult was involved in bizarre and illegal rites including bigamy, incest and child abuse (children of cult members, for example, could be punished by being locked in darkened closets for days on end simply for not being able to recite the Lord's Prayer perfectly). Fairacres was caught in a downward spiral; with each passing year and with each new debased ritual, its reputation became darker and more ominous. Much of the grand beauty that Grace Ceperley had been so proud of was destroyed. Thankfully, Wolsey was exposed in 1960 and fled back to the United States.

After the Temple of the More Abundant Life fragmented and the final remaining members took their strange rites and worship elsewhere, someone had the idea that the mansion would make a suitable residence for students of the newly opened Simon Fraser University. However, students found it difficult to sleep and study in the building owing to paranormal activity, and it seems as though they vented their frustration in vandalism—a bonfire was set on the hardwood floor of the former billiard room, for example, and graffiti was spray painted over the exterior. The university was reluctant to invest in the necessary repairs, and the mansion deteriorated dangerously. Fairacres had suffered badly, both structurally and by reputation, during a half-century of neglect and abuse.

The mansion was rescued when it was purchased by the Municipality of Burnaby in 1966 to be transformed into a community art gallery as part of Canada's Centennial celebrations. After considerable restoration effort and expense, the Burnaby Art Gallery opened in 1967. It was an impressive addition to a growing community, and it soon became a popular landmark.

But if anyone thought the restoration would exorcise the building of its negative spiritual energy, they were mistaken. If anything, the restoration work riled the ghosts further. When floors were ripped up and drywall torn down, the apparitions that had hidden out of sight were released. Ghost sightings and reports of poltergeist activity became common and widespread.

Over the years, staff have heard strange sounds and disembodied voices countless times. Interestingly, unlike in most cases of audible phenomena, when unusual sounds are heard at Fairacres, the temperature dips precipitously, often becoming so cold that teeth chatter and goosebumps form on exposed flesh. One employee who worked in a second-floor office often heard the sounds of footsteps pacing above her head and furniture scraping the floor. It occurred so frequently that as the weeks passed she became accustomed to it. She had no reason to give it much thought at any rate; she simply assumed other staff were working up there. It was only several months later that she discovered the third floor was almost never entered.

But ghostly sounds aren't confined to the third floor. Staff members have heard spectral footsteps walking across the galleries on all of the floors, either before opening or after hours when there should be no one in the building. Investigating the source of the sound, they'd find the gallery empty, and a subsequent search of the entire building revealed that they were indeed alone. "I've heard big, loud bangs when there's nobody left in the building," says one female employee, "and it's really unsettling, because it's so loud and you know there's no one there, so you just want to get out of the building."

The basement has more than its fair share of spectral activity. A male employee was working late one night, alone, in the basement, removing paintings from their frames. It was delicate work that required concentration. Whenever he would put his tools down and turn his back —to go for another painting or reach for his coffee—he would moments later find his tools hung up on the wall several feet away. When he left the room to place the frames in storage, he returned to find the room locked, the padlock on the door swinging as if someone had just left.

Who are these ghosts that lurk restlessly within Fairacres? Psychics and eyewitnesses alike agree there are several, perhaps as many as half a dozen.

Staff members have heard the heart-wrenching sounds of children crying in despair, at least one of whom, according to a visiting psychic, is a girl about 10 years of age whose sadness sometimes pervades the building. Nicole Veira, a longtime employee of the art gallery, often heard the phantom cries of children screaming and crying—well before she knew anything of the somewhat sordid history of the building, which might otherwise have subconsciously coloured her experience. Anyone who heard these heartbreaking cries has never forgotten the pity laced with fear they felt in those moments.

On more than one occasion, staff members have encountered the ethereal children on the third floor. Shy, even fearful, they peer cautiously around corners and run away when spotted. It seems likely that these apparitions are children of the Temple of the More Abundant Life—helpless little ones who were abused and tormented for years by cultists and their deranged leader.

Many people believe the suffering of these young spirits and a desire to comfort them in their tortured afterlife, have brought Grace Ceperley back from the grave. She cared deeply about children, you'll recall, and it's suggested that the suffering of innocents in her beloved home prevents her from resting easily. Others believe that Grace, unwilling to leave her beloved home, has been haunting Fairacres since her death and that her ghost and that of the children just happen to haunt the same building, unaware of each other and unable to interact. Regardless of why Grace has resisted crossing over to the other side, I prefer to think she does indeed provide warmth for the spectral children—it's a comforting thought.

There have been a lot of reports of Grace walking the galleries in a flowing white dress before she disappears through walls. A watchman tells of seeing a woman passing silently from room to room one evening. At first, he thought perhaps the woman was an employee who had unexpectedly stayed late, or worse, someone who had broken into the building. But then he noticed something odd: the mysterious lady floated across the floors

rather than walked upon then, and her form was slightly transparent—glimpses of the room about her could be seen through
her body. She was quite clearly an apparition. The watchman
noted that the spectral woman wore a long, white, flowing dress
that looked like something out of *Downton Abbey*. He watched in
fascination and fear as the figure made her way down the stairs
from the third floor and then vanished through a wall.

Other times, Grace is seen as a misty white figure, distinctly female but ethereal and somewhat blurry, like an out-of-
focus photo. In either event, upon seeing Grace, the eyewitness
is overcome by strong emotions—typically peace and tranquility, but sometimes loneliness and sadness.

An employee named Carol Defina went on record as
having heard Grace Ceperley walking behind her one night
when working alone. To be more accurate, Defina heard the
rustling of Grace's flowing skirt. The sound was unmistakable,
and Defina had worked at the gallery long enough to know
what it meant. A ghost was behind her, perhaps even at her
shoulder, close enough to stretch out an undead arm and place
a chilled hand on Defina. The thought of seeing a ghost terrified
her. She resisted the urge to turn around, too scared of what
she would see, and instead locked her eyes straight ahead as she
raced from the gallery.

Grace may be partnered in the afterlife, as she was in
life, by her husband, Henry. Certainly, several staff members
have come to believe so after catching sight of a distinguished-
looking gentleman in dated formal attire who simply vanishes
into thin air. Those who think the worst of Henry and believe
that he callously refused to follow Grace's dying wish in regards
to Fairacres are of the mind that his spirit has come back from

the grave to apologize and make amends for his wrongdoing. Others, however, are confident he's been drawn back to Fairacres out of love for his home and his wife; he doesn't want to be parted from them, and as long as Grace wanders the halls, he will as well.

Henry makes his presence known throughout the art gallery. His footsteps, louder and more purposeful than Grace's soft and ladylike paces, have been heard walking about after hours, and he has been seen—an elderly man in old-fashioned clothes—standing motionlessly at the top of the staircase, looking down as if to survey his domain from a position of prominence. Some staff believe Henry is the mischievous spirit responsible for moving their tools around in the basement and locking them out of their workroom.

Psychics who have toured the Burnaby Art Gallery believe the ghosts mentioned above may be only the tip of a paranormal iceberg when it comes to lost souls that inhabit the historic building. Over the years, various mediums have picked up the energies of one or more monks, a sickly tuberculosis patient who wants desperately to return home, a mysterious male who is trying to take over the building for undetermined but likely unsavoury reasons, and perhaps even the vile wraith of the self-styled Archbishop John I, William Franklin Wolsey.

With so many spirits competing to carve out their own otherworldly niche, it should come as little surprise that spectral activity in the building was intense—so much so that in recent years, psychics were called in to attempt to assist some of the lost souls in finding their way across to the other side and to whatever rewards await them there. Whether or not any of the ghosts have indeed successfully made the journey, it's been reported that the paranormal activity does seem to have abated somewhat.

See For Yourself

Established in 1967 as a Centennial project, the Burnaby Art Gallery is one of the premier galleries in British Columbia, with a first-rate collection of contemporary art. In addition, in an effort to engage the community and enhance appreciation for the arts, the gallery offers programs designed to interpret works in their exhibitions, from both the City of Burnaby Permanent Collection and works on loan. Hands-on programs and discussions of works on exhibit engage participants and foster both personal expression and the development of technical skills.

Restored to its original 1911 appearance, Fairacres was designated a Heritage Building in 1992. While most people come to the gallery for its artwork, there is little doubt that the building deserves to be considered an exhibit in its own right. With its river rock veranda, beautiful hand-crafted woodwork, stained-glass and tile, the house is one of the finest examples of Edwardian architecture on the Lower Mainland.

Child's Play at the Haliburton Highlands Museum

~

The back roads of central Ontario's Haliburton Highlands, running through hills and valleys filled with lakes and woods and quaint villages, show a breathtaking beauty by day. But when darkness descends, it's a different story. Haliburton is a region steeped in mysterious tales and haunting stories. The supernatural and the sinister are as natural here as pine trees and sandy beaches. Like the hills that hold them, these phantoms are reminders of a sad and often dark past.

Haliburton moves at its own speed, a little slower than the rest of the province; custom and tradition run strong. Stories passed down from generation to generation remain more vibrant and alive than in other regions. The time and mood for the retelling of stories must be just right. That time comes after dinner, when the day begins to wind down and shadows stretch across the land. Sitting on a front porch, around a crackling campfire or in the glow of a fireplace, a quiet settles in. An elder gets a faraway look in his eye, clears his voice and says those magic words: "Did I ever tell you about the time...?" What follows are tales of the macabre, the mysterious and the unexplained—tales that leave the wide-eyed children sitting at the old man's feet leaning in, hanging off every word, enthralled and terrified at the same time. Each one is sure to check under the bed one extra time that night.

Several unsolved mysteries have left generations baffled and provided fodder for heated discussions. Foremost among them is the tale of John Laking.

John Laking was the son of William Laking, one of the most powerful and respected men in early 20th-century Haliburton. By the 1910s, John was increasingly assuming management of his father's lumber company and was elected to the office of reeve of Dysart Township in 1914. But there were whispers that John Laking had a bit of a shady side. When scandal befell the Laking family in 1917, it wasn't altogether a surprise.

The disappearance of John Laking, the son of William Laking (seen here), is one of the enduring mysteries of Haliburton.

John and a companion, Lee Lindsay, embarked on a trip to deliver payroll to the company's logging camp on Drag Lake. The two men climbed into the canoe and paddled out onto the lake, never to be heard from again. When the men didn't return, search parties struggled through the bushes along the lake shore and boats went out onto the lake. Everyone held out hope that the missing men had simply overturned their canoe and would be found shivering but safe. After a few days of fruitless searching, such hopes were dashed and people began to accept that neither man would be found alive.

Finally, an overturned canoe was spotted, and floating nearby was a single cap and a picnic basket. Neither body was ever recovered, even though the lake was dragged and the search for bodies continued on and off for years afterward. Even as funeral services were being held, some tongues were wagging that the men weren't dead but rather had made off with the company payroll. The questions surrounding the men's disappearance never really went away.

Then there is an elusive beast said to hide from mankind in the remote forested hills of Haliburton, retreating to the deepest wilderness after settlers pushed into the region in the late 19th century. The gouger, a species of wild goat, is well adapted to living on hillsides. Legs on one side of its body are shorter than the legs on the opposite side, allowing it to walk on steep slopes and stand comfortably on sloped terrain to graze. This peculiar adaptation means, however, that it can only walk in one direction around a hill; if forced to walk in the other direction, it will topple over.

At one time more numerous than they are today, gougers were domesticated by the first settlers in the region and were crossbred with sheep and regular goats so the offspring could graze more easily on the hills that dominated the settlers' new homesteads. Gouger numbers have dropped precipitously in the century since, largely owing to over-hunting and loss of habitat.

On rare occasions, those venturing into the remote hills might find a trail gouged into the slope by these elusive beasts as they endlessly circle it, or even catch a fleeting glimpse of the mysterious animal itself. Or so go the tall tales told by old-timers, tongue firmly in cheek.

And then there are the numerous ghosts of the highlands that furtively lurk in the region's historic buildings and along its tranquil back roads. Built in 1865, the Dominion Hotel is the oldest standing building in Haliburton County. Doors slam and footsteps are heard when no one is around to cause the sounds, and a ghostly woman has been seen peering out of an upper window toward the river. Legend says she is awaiting the return of her beloved, a lumberjack who worked the river during spring logging drives.

One of the more infamous Haliburton hauntings took place nearly a century ago in the home of the pioneering Stewart family on Head Lake. Lights would flicker over the billiard table; moans would sound ominously in empty rooms; and the keys of the grand piano would jangle under unseen hands. Several people even saw ghostly figures in the home. The house burned in the 1930s—perhaps blessedly.

Martha Perkins, then-editor of the *Haliburton Echo*, contacted me a few years back. This time she didn't have a story to write; instead she had a story to tell. The *Echo*'s offices are located in a 19th-century building that was once the home of

William Laking—the same William Laking whose son John went missing in 1917. Perkins said that she and other newspaper staff members had experienced all manner of paranormal phenomena in their offices, ranging from an uneasy feeling of being watched to unnatural cold spots, and on occasion, they saw a spectre silently climbing the stairs.

These stories and more like them are told alongside more traditional history at the Haliburton Highlands Museum—there's even a taxidermy sidehill gouger greeting guests as they enter. Through exhibits and programming, the museum endeavours to preserve and relate the rich heritage of this unique region of Ontario. Among its extensive collection is said to be a ghost or two, adding to the mysterious lore of Haliburton.

The museum's ghosts confine themselves to the Reid House, one of the historic buildings on site, so most people assume they are tied to that home's past. As such, any discussion of the spirits must begin with a look at the history of the building and its former occupants.

Lured by the promises of the Canadian Land and Emigration Company of Haliburton, in 1871, 50-year-old wheelwright John Russell Reid decided to leave his native England and move to Dysart Township. Accompanying him and equally eager for new opportunities were his wife, Amy, and their 19-year-old son, John Russell Jr. Settling in Haliburton Village, they built a modest cabin and a workshop in what was then little more than a frontier hamlet.

Life in Haliburton in those days was hardscrabble, with only the thinnest veneer of civilization. It proved too much for the elder Reids, who moved back to England less than a decade later. John Russell Jr. remained, however, and in 1882 he married local girl, 30-year-old Janet Clinkscale. That same year, the newlyweds built a comfortable home to replace the Reids' log cabin, a home in which they intended to raise a family and grow old together. And they did just that. Soon it was filled with the sounds of little footsteps at play as first one (Russell), then another (Agnes Amy) and finally a third child (Charlotte Levina) was born.

John Russell Reid was a wagon-maker and woodworker by trade. In addition to wagons and cabinetry, he made snowshoes, toboggans and canoes, as well as small items such as tool handles, veranda posts and yokes. He was also briefly the village constable from 1882 to 1884. John Russell and Janet grew grey together in their home and indeed passed away within its walls.

Russell and Jean Reid

The house then passed to their son Russell, who moved away to Hamilton in search of employment and rented out his home in his absence. In 1924, he married Jean McMullan, a 36-year-old recent immigrant from Ireland. The couple returned to Haliburton at the onset of the Depression and moved into Russell's childhood home. Russell worked as a carpenter and handyman.

A second generation of Reids grew old together in the house, though this couple was not fated to have any children. Russell passed away in the home in 1959, aged 76, and his funeral service was held in the parlour. His widow remained in the home alone for a few more years. Then, when Jean learned the local Rotary Club was considering the establishment of a museum to celebrate the nation's 1967 centennial, she elected to sell her historic home to preserve it and the Reid family legacy. Almost a century old, the Reid House was ideal for the proposed museum.

When it opened on October 23, 1968, the museum proved an immediate success and was embraced by the community. Within a decade, however, the number of donated artifacts had grown so large that the museum was outgrowing the confines of the little house. Clearly a larger museum building was required. Those in charge decided to build a modern, dedicated museum in Glebe Park along the shores of Head Lake. Construction began in 1978. The following year, the old Reid House was moved to join the still-under-construction museum and was refurbished to its early days. Both opened to an excited public on Canada Day, 1980.

The Reid House today looks much as it would have appeared at the time it was inhabited by John Russell and Janet

The innocent charm of the historic Reid House masks ghostly goings-on.

Reid. It still proudly displays the original staircase and the hard-wood floors on which their three children played. And from the day of its opening, several visitors and staff members, both past and present, have had unusual experiences within the home.

One visitor saw a woman in the hallway with her hands on her hips. She didn't seem out of the ordinary at first, except perhaps for the fact that she had an unnerving, faraway look in her eyes. The man thought it a bit strange that the costumed interpreter didn't greet him upon entering as a staff member would typically do, but he shrugged his shoulders and looked around to soak up the charm of the setting. The woman sound-lessly disappeared only moments later. The visitor hadn't seen her go, nor did he hear her footsteps or the groaning of floor-boards that would have signalled her leaving. In retrospect, the stern look on the woman's face and her hands-on-hips pose gave the visitor the impression that the apparition was upset at the intrusion of his entrance.

That summer day marked the only sighting of this spectral woman—whoever she might be. The more active spirit, explains museum director Kate Butler, seems to be that of a young child.

"Just this past summer we had a family with a four-year-old son visit the museum. We were too busy to give them a guided tour, so they headed out on their own to check out the Reid House. When they came back, the son told me he saw a little boy in the house. There was no one else over there at the time, so it couldn't have been a real boy, but I believe he saw something," says Butler.

Other visitors have told Butler of similar experiences. "While I was guiding one woman through the home, she told me she sensed a presence there. She didn't elaborate and I didn't follow up, unfortunately."

Several people have encountered this youngster in one form or another over the years. The Sloan family visited the museum while vacationing in Haliburton one summer. The excursion was an opportunity to get their three children away from the cottage for a few hours; after more than a week on the lake and in the woods, the kids needed a new stimulus. If they could be exposed to some history at the same time, so much the better. While in the Reid House, the parents heard giddy children's laughter filtering down from upstairs. They smiled at one another, pleased that their kids were enjoying themselves. Smiles faded quickly, however, when their little ones appeared behind them. The parents exchanged a questioning look: if their own three children were still on the first floor, who were the children playing upstairs? They thought they were alone in the house. The Sloans climbed the staircase to find out, but it appeared the rooms were empty. Perhaps the ghostly children were playing a game of hide-and-seek with the living.

"Tasha," a woman who asked that her real name be withheld, believes that's exactly the case. She came to this conclusion after a school trip to the museum several decades ago. That day, she received an education in the horrors of the supernatural world.

"I didn't really want to go on the class trip to the museum. But it meant we got out of school, and that's always a good thing. I never really believed in ghosts or the supernatural, but when I pass a cemetery I always walk on the other side of the street. I refuse to walk under ladders or cross a black cat, and when I enter some place that's supposed to be haunted, I always say a respectful prayer for the dead. Why take chances, right? But that day at the museum there was no reason to suspect the old Reid House was haunted, so I neglected to say my prayer. I guess that was a mistake."

The daytrip began innocently enough. As a child, Tasha didn't appreciate the Reid House for the treasure it was. To her, it was just an old house that reminded her of the one her grandparents used to live in. At one point, she heard soft nursery rhymes filtering down the stairs. She glanced up a saw a strange boy sitting on the landing above. He was freckle-faced and aged about five, and when he smiled there was a gap where he was missing two front teeth. Tasha and the boy made eye contact, and then he was gone.

"I was scared. I ran and told my best friend. I wanted her to go upstairs with me to see if the boy had just run off down the hall. She just rolled her eyes and laughed. She didn't believe me. I guess I don't blame her," Tasha says. "I tried hard to put it out of my mind, and after a while I pretty much did. The remainder of the day passed normally."

And that was that. The experience—startling as it may have been—was over. Or was it?

Tasha was awoken later that night by the sound of nursery rhymes in her bedroom. She lifted her head from her pillow and saw the same gap-toothed boy standing at the foot of her bed. His mouth didn't move, yet still Tasha heard the soothing nursery rhymes. She screamed. When she did, the boy started to transform; his bright, playful eyes were replaced by dark, sunken holes, and he was now covered in cobwebs and dust.

Tasha dove under the blankets. She cowered there for what seemed like hours but in retrospect was probably only a few minutes before she tentatively pulled the blankets down low enough to peer over the top. The boy was gone.

It took Tasha years to get over the experience. For a long time, thinking about that youthful apparition terrified her. But now, doing so fills her with sadness. She believes the boy hadn't intended to frighten her but instead was lonely for a playmate and had followed her home to continue their friendship.

Kate Butler hasn't experienced anything unusual herself during the four years since she took on the position of museum director, but the former professor of folklore does believe in the existence of ghosts. "My question isn't whether there's a ghost in the Reid House, but who he might be. That's the mystery," she explains, noting that history doesn't make any suggestions as to the ghost boy's identity because we're not aware of any inhabitants whose lives were tragically cut short.

"There is one possibility that I can think of: when Russell Reid was living in Hamilton, he rented out the home and we don't know anything about the renters. Maybe the child of a renter died in the home, but I guess we may never know." Sometimes it's this sort of mystery that makes for a great ghost story—the kind that makes us ask questions as well as sends shivers down our spines.

Legends and campfire tales tell of individuals too evil to die, too stubborn or too full of pride to cross over to the other side, too resentful of lost opportunities to rest easily after a life unfulfilled. These lost souls become restless spirits that plague shadowy back roads, dark crypts and, of course, buildings weathered by time and age, terrifying unsuspecting mortals. But while such eerie entities are staples of fiction and film, not every ghost is so dark and festering.

Indeed, the Reid House at Haliburton Highlands Museum is haunted by an innocent, playful child. We don't know who he was in life, but we know his story is a sad one because his time to leave this earth and be reunited with his family is long past. How long will this lad remain at the Reid House, a lost soul wandering aimlessly down hallways and smiling at guests in the hopes of enticing someone—anyone—to play with him? We can only hope that one day soon he will realize he no longer belongs to this world and will cross over to be with his parents. Until then, maybe you could spend some time playing with him when next you visit the museum.

See For Yourself

The Haliburton Highlands Museum was founded in 1967 as a Canadian Centennial project whose mandate was to preserve, promote and celebrate the history of Haliburton Village and Dysart Township. Over the years it has grown substantially from a single home to a complex of buildings.

The museum's main exhibit building has two floors and houses thematic exhibits related specifically to Native peoples, settlers, lumbermen and the rise of tourism after the arrival of the railways. It quickly becomes apparent how hard life could be in this early period, when Haliburton was a frontier not yet fully tamed. The building also features a variety of frequently changing displays, focusing on such subjects as children's toys or 19th-century women's clothing.

Behind this building stands the Victorian-era Reid House, which has often been referred to the as the museum's largest artifact. A beautiful period home, it has been restored to a late 1890s, early 1900s appearance, when John and Janet Reid would have been residing in it. Vividly brought back to life with appropriate furnishings and artifacts—including a number of Reid-family pieces—the building hosts many demonstrations and events, such as pioneer cooking.

Down a quiet country lane sits a recreated pioneer homestead, depicting the modest and often harsh existence faced by most settlers in early Haliburton. The farmstead consists of an 1870s log cabin, a log barn of similar era containing the tools and equipment a farmer would have used to try to transform the imposing forests and rocky soil into thriving fields of crops, and a blacksmith shop where a craftsman works away.

"We have a full event schedule; there's always something going on here," enthuses manager Kate Butler. "One of our favourites is our maple syrup festival. We tap our own trees and, over March break, boil it down in the same manner as the early settlers. We also partner with Heritage Boat Tours to host summer tours that focus on the development of the tourism industry, because most of the resorts and lodges are gone now. And of course we do a lot of children's programming because we want to get kids interested in history early."

It seems there is something for everyone.

Cobalt's Ghostly Bunker Military Museum

~

For most people, death is a release—a passage into the just rewards of the afterlife. Yet not everyone rests easy. Some, usually those whose end came prematurely, who left behind unfinished business or who died in some tragic manner, stubbornly refuse to cross over to the other side. It should come as little surprise that warfare should result in an explosion of restless dead. In every conflict in human history, young men (and women) died never having experienced all that life promises. When even a fraction of these fallen soldiers rise from their graves as lost souls, they create a veritable army of spectres and wraiths haunting blood-soaked battlefields around the world, to say nothing of the many museums that commemorate these clashes of arms.

Cobalt's Bunker Military Museum is one such location where the wars of the past continue to haunt the present. Little known outside of northeastern Ontario but one of the most impressive small-town museums anywhere in the province, it boasts a stunning range of artifacts from across the world and throughout the 20th century. If, as many parapsychologists theorize, particularly strong emotions can seep into physical items to permanently stain them, imagine how many of the items in this museum's collection have been tainted by the horrors of war. No need to wonder—just ask the staff.

"I wasn't a believer when I came here, but I now know there's something beyond life. There have been too many unexplainable events here to dismiss it," says Marg Harrison, president of the Bunker Military Museum Board. She believes that some of these hauntings are, naturally, linked to the artifacts on display, while others may perhaps be linked to the building itself, which is a historic artifact in its own right.

The Bunker Military Museum is located within the Fraser Hotel, which was, at one time, undoubtedly the most impressive and attractive building in Cobalt—the pride of a community growing in wealth and confidence. In 1909, Cobalt was nearing the height of its fortunes; in that year alone its mines produced some 25 million ounces of silver, making the community the richest silver-producing area in the vast British Empire. That same year, the building that today is best remembered as the Fraser Hotel was built. In its original form, it was the Royal Stock Exchange, designed to facilitate the tracking and trading of the silver being pulled from the ground. Oddly enough, while investors and stock traders were conducting business on the top floors, dynamite for use in the mines was being manufactured in a munitions factory in the basement.

A short time later, the building was transformed into a luxurious hotel patronized by wealthy mine owners when inspecting their holdings in town. Several foreign dignitaries stayed there while touring the town, and well-known European theatrical performers called the establishment home when their shows made stops in Cobalt. The hotel was a swank place where members of upper-class society could feel right at home. No money was spared in its design and furnishing, and the hotel even boasted a mauve-coloured glass sidewalk that was illuminated by lights from beneath, a feature otherwise found only in the classiest spots in New York, Chicago, London and Paris.

By the dawn of the 21st century, the Fraser Hotel was a mockery of its former self, sitting abandoned and derelict. It was whispered that ghosts would assault anyone who entered. People shunned it.

Since then, plans have developed that, if fully realized, will transform the historic building into a centrepiece of the community once more. It is currently home to the Bunker Military Museum, which moved from the former railway station into the hotel's basement in November 2012, and two dozen apartments occupy the upper floors. Several ideas are being floated about to fill the empty main floor once occupied by the hotel bar. With revived fortunes, will the ghosts lurking in the cavernous depths of the Fraser Hotel find peace at last? Not so far, according to museum staff.

Spirits of wars of the past haunt the present at the Bunker Military Museum.

Marg Harrison has spent more time in the museum than nearly anyone, and she's had her share of unusual experiences within the historic building—experiences that have changed her view of life and death. "I had heard stories over the years that the Fraser Hotel was haunted, but as a retired nurse I'm a very black and white person. I believe what I can see and touch; I believe in fact. I never believed in ghosts, so I wasn't scared about being in the building," she explains.

Marg threw her herself into the task of establishing a volunteer museum board and, after spending hours upon hours in the Fraser Hotel, soon found herself questioning her previous notions regarding the paranormal. "The supernatural events began pretty modestly," she admits. "I often answer the phone, and if I take a message, I always leave it nearby, either to give to someone later or perhaps to remind me to return a call when I get a free moment. There were times when I'd go back later in the day and the note would be missing, only to later turn up mysteriously in another room. I'm a very organized person and don't misplace things, so I know I'm not absentmindedly leaving the notes around the museum. I couldn't explain it."

Although these events were perplexing, Marg remembers it was the 2014 Thanksgiving weekend when she began to seriously consider the existence of ghosts. Because other board members had family members coming in from out of town for the holiday, Marg generously offered to operate the museum all three days that weekend.

Entering the building that Saturday morning, she performed the usual opening routine, which included turning on all the lights and ensuring certain interior doors were locked so that visitors can't get into offices or other off-limit areas. This day would be anything but routine, however. When she grabbed hold of the handle of the electrical room door—which is almost never used and should always be locked—Marg was surprised to find it open. Perplexed, she went to the office, retrieved the key and made certain to lock the door. At four that afternoon, when closing the museum for the evening, she tried the door again and was stunned to find it unlocked. Again, she got the key and locked the door.

Returning Sunday morning to open the museum, Marg once more found the electrical room door unlocked. Frustrated and now a bit uneasy, she got the key and locked the door. Sure enough, it was once again open when the museum closed for the night. Now stricken with disbelief, the door that wouldn't remain locked was all she could think about on the way home.

The conversation that night between Marg and her husband centred on the perplexing mystery of the last two days. They both took some time to consider the circumstances and tried but failed to find a rational explanation. Finally, Marg's husband suggested that she simply tell the ghost in no uncertain terms to leave the door locked. Although dubious, Marg was desperate and agreed to try.

When she returned to the museum on Monday morning, Marg stepped through the front door and paused to steady her nerves. She took a deep breath and in her most authoritative voice said, "Ok, Fred" (she doesn't know where the name Fred came from; it simply blurted out), "enough is enough. The electrical room door has to be locked at all times so kids don't get in there. It's a safety issue, so leave it alone."

Nervously, afraid of what she would find, Marg then made her way towards the electrical room. To her surprise and relief, the scolding seemed to work. The door was locked that morning and was still locked when she left that night. Indeed, there hasn't been a problem with the door unlocking of its own accord since.

On another occasion, a mother and her two children— one about three years old, the other a girl of about 12—visited the museum. Marg gave them a quick tour and encouraged the kids to try spelling their names with the working World War I Morse code machine on display in the communications gallery.

When Marg heard the distinctive sound of the Morse code machine clicking away, she smiled happily to herself, pleased that children were experiencing history first hand. But moments later, the museum echoed with high-pitched screams of pure terror. Marg was stunned to see the 12-year-old girl racing from the communications gallery at full speed, her eyes as big as saucers. She ran straight for the exit and was pushing her way through the doors when Marg reached the terrified girl and tried desperately to calm her. The girl wrapped her arms around Marg and clung to her for long minutes, her heart pounding in her chest, moans escaping from her throat.

When Marg's soothing words had finally calmed the girl enough for her to be able to speak, she explained what had happened. She had just entered the communications room when the Morse code machine began working by itself, tapping away as if under the fingers of an unseen hand.

Marg has actually seen the museum's ghost on a few occasions. One of the exhibits is known as the parade ground because it features 65 mannequin-soldiers in full uniform, lined up side by side as if standing on parade. Several times now, Marg has pulled up short upon seeing a dark figure standing in the middle of the room. The figure looms dark and ominous, motionless and utterly silent. Although otherwise unthreatening, the spirit seems to embody the inevitability of death and always leaves Marg shaken.

Marg isn't the only staff member to encounter something unusual in the museum. "There are all sorts of weird noises and sounds around here that are unexplainable," says curator-manager Dan Larocque. "I literally designed the museum myself, everything from the placement of power outlets to lighting, so I know almost everything about it, yet there are still sounds I can't identify. I'll hear something strange and spend a lot of time trying to find a logical cause, but often I can't find one. It can freak you out if you think too much about it."

So many of us have had moments when the dark closes in and you just know that someone or something terrible is watching you from the shadows. You don't just feel it—you instinctively know it. Your heart pounds in your chest as your pulse races. You have to do something. But what? Our natural instinct is to get out of there as fast as possible. It's a feeling Dan knows all too well.

"I'm in the museum alone a lot while closing up at night, and after the lights are turned off it gets really dark—there are no windows to allow in streetlight or the glow of the moon. When I walk through the gallery to leave I often feel like something is watching me from the darkness. I keep my head down, my eyes on the floor and never flash my light anywhere but straight ahead. I don't want to see what might be in the shadows," he says seriously.

One day after hours, Dan found himself adjusting the uniform on a mannequin located near the front of the gallery. Behind him, at the far end of the hall, was a maintenance door that accessed the elevator shaft. He had his back to the hall when he suddenly heard footsteps directly behind him. He froze.

The footsteps were so distinct, so loud that whoever—or whatever—caused them must have been standing right behind him. Dan heard the footsteps receding down the hall and saw the hall's motion-sensitive lights turning on as the footsteps passed. Breathing hard, his heart pounding, Dan was too scared to move. Then the maintenance door slammed open and shut. Dan couldn't believe it. That door is extremely heavy. Dan is a big guy, and even he can barely open it even throwing his full weight behind the effort. Completely unnerved by the experience, Dan hurriedly shut up the museum and put the restless spirit behind him.

Most artifacts exhibited in the museum naturally attract interest, but there's one that seems to repel it: a Russian soldier's World War II helmet. There's nothing outwardly unusual about it, yet many people admit to feeling uncomfortable in its presence. Perhaps it repels because it reminds us of the most destructive war in human history, or maybe because it was worn by a soldier serving the cold and merciless Soviet regime. But somehow it exudes an ominous and vaguely frightening aura.

Dan knows people have good reason to be repelled by the helmet. He recalls the day years ago, back when the museum was located in the Cobalt train station, when he knew there was something very wrong with the helmet.

"It was strapped to a mannequin head and placed on a table. I went for lunch and returned to find the helmet cocked sideways on the head. The helmet weighs 8 pounds and was strapped tightly to the head, so it couldn't move on its own. In fact, I had to really tug it to straighten it again. I was the only one there and the only one with keys, so it's not possible that someone was playing a joke on me. The same thing happened several other times. That helmet freaks me out," Dan says.

The restless spirit of at least one soldier wanders through the exhibit halls at the Bunker Military Museum. Although his physical remains lie in a cemetery, perhaps even oversees if he fell in battle, his tortured spirit has followed the artifacts to Cobalt. His clinging to the mortal realm chains him in a dungeon of the afterlife, preventing him from finding any peace. Sadly, it seems the ghost (or perhaps, ghosts) is destined never to be mustered out of service and is doomed to linger among artifacts that remind him of the horrors of war. And on certain nights, the undead soldier reminds the world that he is still there.

See For Yourself

The Bunker Military Museum has come a long way from its origins as the private collection of Jim Jones, a World War II veteran who returned home from active duty with an assortment of artifacts and memorabilia. Today, the museum boasts 5300 square feet of exhibit space, making it one of the largest galleries in northern Ontario and one of the premier tourist attractions in Cobalt. The collection consists of hundreds of artifacts from the Boer War, both World Wars, the Korean War and present-day conflicts and includes items from around the world. Uniforms, weaponry, medals and other forms of military memorabilia from Canada, America, Germany, Italy, Russia, France and many other nations are engagingly displayed throughout a variety of themed galleries.

Highlights include the communications gallery, with its working World War I-era military Morse code machine where you can type out a hurried battlefield message, the parade ground hall of mannequins outfitted in resplendent uniforms and a recreated Western Front trench where visitors gain a sense of front line conditions during World War I in France. The Bunker Military Museum is truly one of Ontario's hidden gems.

Notes on Sources

Boyle, Terry. *Haunted Ontario 4: Encounters with Ghostly Shadows, Apparitions and Spirits.* Toronto: Dundurn, 2015

Buse, Dieter K. and Graeme S. Mount. *Come on Over! Northeastern Ontario A to Z.* Sudbury: Scrivener Press, 2011.

Carnochan, Janet. *History of Niagara. Belleville*: Mika Publishing, 1973 (originally published 1914).

Cobalt Historical Society. *The Heritage Silver Trail.* Cobalt: The Highway Bookshop, 2000.

Colombo, John Robert. *Mysteries of Ontario.* Toronto: Hounslow Press, 1999.

Dale, Ronald J. *Niagara-on-the-Lake: Its Heritage and Its Festival.* Toronto: James Lorimer and Company, 1999.

Da Silva, Maria and Andrew Hind. *Cottage Country Ghosts.* Edmonton: Ghost House Books, 2010.

———. *Ghosts of Niagara-on-the-Lake.* Toronto: Dundurn, 2009.

———. *Ghost Stories of the First World War.* Edmonton: Ghost House Books, 2014.

———. *Ghost Stories of the War of 1812.* Edmonton: Ghost House Books, 2012.

———. *Haunted Ontario Lakes.* Edmonton: Ghost House Books, 2015.

———. *More Ontario Ghost Stories.* Edmonton: Ghost House Books, 2012.

———. *Muskoka: Enchanting Stories of Ontario's Cottage Country.* Edmonton: Folklore Publishing, 2013.

Fancy, Peter. *Temiskaming Treasure Trails.* Cobalt: The Highway Bookshop, 1993.

Komus, Matthew. *Haunted Winnipeg: Ghost Stories from the Heart of the Continent.* Winnipeg: Great Plains Publications, 2014.

Leslie, Mark and Jenny Jelen. *Spooky Sudbury: True Tales of the Eerie and Unexplained.* Toronto: Dundurn, 2016.

Mika, Nick and Gary Thompson. *Black Creek Pioneer Village.* Toronto: Natural Heritage Books, 2000.

Oickle, Vernon. *Ghost Stories of the Maritimes.* Edmonton: Ghost House Books, 2001.

———. *Ghost Stories of the Maritimes, Volume 2.* Edmonton: Ghost House Books, 2001.

Savoie, John. *Shadows of Niagara.* Niagara Falls: Self-published, 2005.

Smith, Barbara. *Ghost Stories and Mysterious Creatures of British Columbia.* Edmonton: Ghost House Books, 1999.

———. *Ghost Stories of Alberta.* Toronto: Hounslow Press, 1988.

Upton, Kyle. *Niagara's Ghosts Two.* Niagara-on-the-Lake: Self-published, 2004.

Wallace, C.M. and Ashley Thomson. *Sudbury: Railtown to Regional Capital.* Toronto: Dundurn, 1996.

Watson, John C. *Ghost Stories and Legends of Prince Edward Island.* Toronto: Hounslow Press, 1988.

About the Author

Andrew Hind is a freelance writer who specializes in history and travel. He has a passion for bringing to light unusual stories, little-known episodes in history and fascinating locations few people know about. Andrew is the author of more than 20 books and has contributed numerous articles to national and international magazines and newspapers, including *Muskoka Life*, *Lakeland Boating*, *Canada's History*, *History Magazine*, *Wild West* and others. He conducts historical talks and tours that help people connect to the past, and, with Maria Da Silva, ghost tours.

Andrew now resides in Bradford, Ontario. You can follow him on Twitter @discoveriesAM.